Job Market: Survival Guide in 2012 & Beyond

ISBN: 978-0-578-09353-6 (paper book)
ISBN: 978-0-578-09477-9 (e-book)

I0122644

Chapter 1: Introduction

Summary: enumerate the triggers for writing this book; enumerate the focus, structure and approach in this book.

During the 25 years in mentorship, consulting and project management roles, I have the opportunity to plan, implement and document various strategies of preparing for, keeping and transitioning from jobs to other jobs in several industries – healthcare, banking, finance, semi-conductor, retail, aerospace, automotive, telecommunications, oil, federal/state/county/city governments, entertainment, and transportation - among others.

The primary reason for writing this book - is personal and very to close to home. I have lived through the debilitating, paralyzing and traumatic tragedies of long-term unemployment or underemployment of my peers, associates, friends, family members and immediate circles. As of September 2011, according to the U.S. Bureau of Labor Statistics and International Labor Organization, the number of unemployed individuals in the U.S. is at **14 million**, world-wide is at **220 million**. If you factor in those who are long-term unemployed and underemployed, the figures are at least double these numbers.

The second reason – is most programs on this subject have been focused on resume writing and interview skills, which are at the later stages of the job search and survival process; and, there is a lack of coverage at the front-end like acquiring good working habits while in the formative stages, and focusing on industries and specializations that will provide the optimal promise and options. This book is focused at the front-end stages of the process, where most of the pivotal decisions and preparations occur, and which will drive what options and what contents end up being in the resume at a later time. Using an analogy, the front-end stages of a job search and survival process is the equivalent of baking the cake, while the later stages which include resumes and interviews being the icing in the cake. Eventually, the cake and the icing should converge and are usually evaluated as a package, but neither is appealing without the other.

The third reason – is concern on the catastrophic failure of governance resulting in the 2008 global financial meltdown. Primarily because of this, and exacerbated by the ongoing stalemate in Washington D.C., we lost millions of jobs, while the competition has been systematically leaving us behind, and those who wish us harm have been rejoicing the implosion from within our increasingly fragmented country.

Several of the strategies in this book are referred to by various descriptive terms, such as: **"Cradle to Grave"**; **"Feast and Famine"**; **"Charge of the Light Brigade"**; **"Last Stand at Thermopylae"**; etc. Several of these strategies have been anachronistic for decades but continued to be practiced with unintended and tragic consequences that need not happen.

To illustrate and reinforce how to best apply the **"best practices and lessons learned"** from this book, and at the risk of oversimplifying an otherwise complex process with various dependencies, Chapters 8, 9, 10 and 11 depict scenarios that are based on real-life cases without disclosure of names, places or dates. I wanted you to pick something from this book that could complement your repertoire of tools to compete in today's increasingly competitive and, in several cases, overcrowded and shrinking job market.

Due to the current economic climate and the **"time sensitive"** nature of the information being shared, the urgency of publishing this book takes precedence over additional refinements and aesthetics. Those refinements will be addressed separately and at future revisions. In so doing, I hope that this will benefit those who could use the information immediately. For some, it could even be a game changer.

For those who lost their jobs before, or just about to lose their jobs, several chapters in this book will resonate and endear in ways that will not make any sense to those who have not lost their jobs before, or those unable to relate to the crippling consequences of losing jobs during severe and prolonged economic downturns.

Regardless, if you need encouragement or could use a different perspective and approach, please read through and click through the links in Appendix C: Verses to Cheer You Up, Appendix D: Movies to Cheer You Up, and Appendix E: Music to Cheer You Up in this book, including listening to the music and watching the movies. Some of the people who did, were reminded of those times long gone, and experienced reflections and encounters that are enlightening, endearing and lasting to this day. I would like to point out that these Appendices and other sections referencing URLs are best read and experienced in an e-book or electronic format compared to that of a printed book. This is due to the use of hyperlinks that allows you to click back and forth among various references. If you wish to receive an updated list of these hyperlinks, please send an email message to jobsurvival-subscribe@yahoogroups.com, or JobSurvival2012.Beyond@gmail.com.

This book neither guarantees nor promises that you will get and keep a job. What this book does, is if you follow the guidelines in this book in its entirety, your chances of getting and keeping a job is much more structured, focused and sustainable.

This book includes the following:

- Chapter 1: Introduction
- Chapter 2: Why a Job is Important
- Chapter 3: Audience and Stakeholders
- Chapter 4: Current Economic Conditions and Expectations
- Chapter 5: Then and Now
- Chapter 6: Guidelines for Keeping a Job
- Chapter 7: "Cradle to Grave" Preparations
- Chapter 8: Scenario - What to Do When You Are Laid off or About to Be Laid Off?
- Chapter 9: Scenario – I will Stay Where I am
- Chapter 10: Scenario – Retooling and Transitioning to Another Job
- Chapter 11: Scenario - What to do When You Are a Happy Camper?
- Chapter 12: Summary
- Appendix A: 2008 thru 2018 U.S. Job Projections
- Appendix B: International Unemployment Rates and Employment Indexes, Seasonally Adjusted
- Appendix C: Verses to Cheer You Up
- Appendix D: Movies to Cheer You Up
- Appendix E: Music to Cheer You Up
- Appendix F: Job Search Resources
- Appendix G: Une Journée dans la vie d'un Imbécile: 8/26/2011
- Appendix H: Expand Your Horizon

Workplace politics and personalities are out-of-scope for this book.

Finally, this book is not intended to cover visionaries and captains of industries – like Steve Jobs, Bill Gates and others. They and other topics will be covered in "Job Market: Innovators, Stakeholders & Infrastructure", "Job Market: Family and Support System" and "Job Market: The Retired, Disadvantaged and Marginalized" at a future time.

Chapter 2: Why a Job is Important

Summary: the job that we have or don't have defines who we are and what we can be.

Preparing for and keeping a job is a personal and professional choice. Generally, it is easier to find a job when one has a job, compared to when one does not have a job. Without a stable job, one cannot plan. If one cannot plan, one has limited options.

A job is not entertainment; unless you are independently wealthy or blessed, you need a job to pay the bills. I do not know of anybody who has ever claimed that he or she has a sustainable dream job. Once you have a stable job, then, by all means pursue your dreams in parallel, but not the other way around.

A stable and endearing job is key to **"self esteem"**, stability and relationship with your family, peers and the community. Failure to address this on a decisive and timely basis will result in self-imposed marginalization and being relegated into to the so called "underclass" that will have lasting effects and will transcend generations and boundaries.

When a person is unemployed or underemployed for a long time, there is a long-term impact on one's psyche and ability to normally interact with others and prepare for the next cycle. A damaged **"self-esteem"** is manifested during the interview for a job, personal relationships, or other settings.

If you are independently wealthy or blessed, this book is probably a mere curiosity to you.

Chapter 3: Audience and Stakeholders

Summary: Preparing for, capturing and keeping a stable job require family, community and multi-disciplinary support.

The target audience and stakeholders of this book are:

- Those who are unemployed
- Those who are underemployed
- Those who are currently employed and preparing for contingencies
- Those in a career transition
- Retirees who find it necessary to return to the job market
- Supervisors and managers
- Parents or guardians providing career guidance to their children
- Counselors, advisers and teachers providing career guidance to their students
- Mentors and mentees
- High school students
- College students
- Researchers
- Funders
- Public officials and policy makers
- Family members and loved ones of the stakeholders above

Chapter 4: Current Economic Conditions and Expectations

Summary: this chapter enumerates the harsh economic realities of our times and the immediate future. We just avoided a 1930's-magnitude global depression, but this is no consolation to those who have been displaced or will be displaced. This chapter is an imperative reading for context and to properly craft your job search and survival strategy.

We take it for granted the myriads of blessings immediately after WW II. This includes an abundance of job options and projects to go around in most specializations and industries.

With the global financial meltdown of 2008, circumstances are drastically different from those of previous decades and generations. There are projections that the new norm will be 12% unemployment or higher, compared to the 7% average unemployment prior to the 2008 meltdown - in a gradually disappearing middle-class environment.

In assessing your job and career development prospects, consider the following context:

- Geithner sounds alarm on Europe

  http://money.cnn.com/2011/09/24/markets/geithner_debt/index.htm?hpt=hp_t2

- Treasury Department chief economist Alan Krueger said that household net wealth fell by approximately $17 trillion between 2007 and 2009 due to the financial crisis. That is a lot of household purchasing power being lost and do you really believe that $2 trillion of stimulus could make up the difference?

  http://thehill.com/blogs/on-the-money/801-economy/95689-financial-crisis-cost-households-17-trillion-treasury-official-says

- Total properties receiving foreclosure filings would have easily exceeded 3 million in 2010 had it not been for the fourth-quarter drop in foreclosure activity — triggered primarily by the continuing controversy surrounding foreclosure documentation and procedures that prompted many major lenders to temporarily halt some foreclosure proceedings . . .

http://www.foreclosurebusinessnews.com/home-foreclosure-statistics-for-first-time-in-history-foreclosures-top-1-million-thats-not-the-worst-of-it/

- According to the former U.S. Comptroller General (GAO), David Walker, the credit crunch could portend a far greater fiscal crisis; and on CNN, he said that the United States is "underwater to the tune of $50 trillion" in long-term obligations.

  http://en.wikipedia.org/wiki/David_M._Walker_(U.S._Comptroller_General)

- In California, the most recent federal budget compromise cutbacks of 2011 is estimated to cut at least $10 billion of federal funding each year. Adding insult to injury, the state of California has its own budget woes.

- Unfunded Pension liabilities: States - $3 trillion; Municipalities - $574 billion

  http://www.washingtonpost.com/wp-dyn/content/article/2010/10/12/AR2010101200044.html

  http://www.businessinsider.com/scary-facts-about-the-coming-pension-crisis-2010-8#

- On the recently announced 30,000 layoff at Bank of America (BofA). For each BofA laid off employee, there could be 5 or more contractors laid off but which there are no press release announcement made. This is the multiplier effect of those announced layoffs and could vary from company to company and industry to industry.

  http://articles.latimes.com/2011/sep/10/business/la-fi-bank-america-jobs-20110910

  http://www.dailyjobcuts.com/

- There has been a pattern reduced business activities in the clinics of physicians and dentists, offices of lawyers and accountants, and other small to medium businesses. These are not usually covered by the press but they are there.

  http://www.dailyjobcuts.com/

- The U.S. winding down its role in Iraq and Afghanistan. This means hundreds of thousands of veterans will soon be joining an already flooded unemployed or underemployed work force.

  http://slatest.slate.com/posts/2011/09/26/army_troop_drawdw on_lt_gen_thomas_bostick_outlines_plan_to_cut_5.html

- The next round of federal cut back of more than 1 trillion will further impact the unemployment market.

- Consider the following in the case of Apple. Apple has 50,000 employees in the U.S and has 1 million employees in China (through Apple and its suppliers).

  http://slavin.tumblr.com/post/6609595776/apple-employees-50-000-people-foxconn-employs

  http://en.wikipedia.org/wiki/Foxconn

- I am coming across more and more graduates taking their 2nd, 3rd and 4th majors or specializations because there are no jobs in their originally chosen disciplines, or they do not like what are available in those disciplines, or both. By the way, I have gone through this process several times myself.

- There is a trend where more companies are hiring employees for a duration of between 6 months to 2 years only. At the end of this duration, the employees are terminated and replaced by the next batch of employees who will work between 6 months to 2 years, then terminated, and replaced by the next batch, and the cycle continues. The concept of a permanent employee is lost in this model. In most industries, there is a trend that new and younger employees, performing the same tasks, are not eligible to the same pay and benefits as previous workers.

http://www.pewcenteronthestates.org/initiatives_detail.aspx?initiativeID=61599

http://www.businessinsurance.com/article/20100711/ISSUE01/307119995#

- PBS.org - "Can America's Unemployed Fill American Jobs?" 2 experts looked at the extent to which high unemployment is structural and how much is cyclical. What are the so called "bubble jobs and jobless recovery"?

  http://video.pbs.org/video/2119473230#

- PBS.org - Single, Jobless and Living at Home: Will Economy Create a 'Lost Generation'? Employment among young adults between the ages of 16 to 29 was at its lowest levels since the end of World War II. Just 55 percent were employed, compared with 67 percent in 2000; Nearly 6 million Americans between the ages of 25 to 34 lived at their parents' homes last year.

  http://www.pbs.org/newshour/rundown/2011/09/rough-times-for-young-adults-in-americas.html?utm_source=Facebook&utm_medium=fanpage&utm_campaign=pbs

- Without a job, California woman forced to live a lie

  http://www.cnn.com/2011/IREPORT/09/24/new.face.of.poverty.unemployed/index.html?hpt=hp_c1

- The Job Market is Frozen for Everyone

  http://www.npr.org/blogs/money/2011/10/07/141147858/the-job-market-is-frozen-for-everyone

- Poverty pervades the suburbs

http://money.cnn.com/2011/09/23/news/economy/poverty_suburbs/index.htm?iid=Popular

- **Boomers' 'Delusion' About Health In Retirement**

  http://www.npr.org/2011/09/28/140853479/boomers-delusion-about-health-in-retirement

- **'Retirement Heist': How Firms Trimmed Pensions**

  http://www.npr.org/2011/09/29/140344871/retirement-heist-how-firms-trimmed-pensions

- **'Grandparents raising Grandchildren'**

  http://www.childwelfare.gov/preventing/supporting/resources/grandparents.cfm

  http://www.grandparenting.org/Grandparents_Raising_Grandchildren.htm

  http://www.raisingyourgrandchildren.com/States/California.htm

  http://www.aarp.org/relationships/friends-family/grandfacts-sheets/

The aggregate impact of these developments and realities means that things are going to get very nasty and worse before it gets any better for a long time.

Chapter 5: Then and Now

Summary: the world we live in today is far different from the world where we grew up at. The sooner we come to terms with this reality, the more realistic our plans and expectations will be.

In a seminar, the cost of living 50 years ago was presented. A husband worked for General Motors or General Electric; the wife stayed at home and cared for the children; 3 of their children finished college and got decent jobs; the husband and wife owned a house and cars; they participated in church and community events; and, they lived and retired comfortably.

Prior to the financial meltdown in 2008, how many families do you know today who closely fit this profile of a household? How about after factoring the Economic Conditions and Expectations enumerated in Chapter 4 of this book, how many families do you know today who closely fit this profile?

The point here is in today's environment, the following are probable scenarios:

- If you are currently employed, unemployment or underemployment is possible for reasons that have nothing to do with your job performance.
- If you are retired, your social security and pension might be insufficient to support your lifestyle, requiring you to seek a part-time or full-time job.
- If others depend on your income, you have bigger challenges to manage.

The following are several of the most common triggers for unemployment or underemployment:

- If it is government agency or a project funded by a government agency, funding is cut.
- The company is closing shop due to competition that priced out the products and services of this company.
- The company is engaged in a cost saving program and decided to outsource jobs – onshore, or off-shore, or both. Only minimally paid and less attractive jobs remain.
- Company is relocating to another state or country.

- The company is changing, and require a different breed of workers that overall are cheaper.
- The company is acquired, or merging, or consolidating, and there are duplication or job functions.
- Compensation package for jobs is not sustainable.
- Employee is unable to relocate.
- Performance reasons.
- Personality conflicts.
- Incompatible value.

From the hiring companies' perspective, the following are the most frequent parameters for evaluating a candidate for hiring and job retention purposes. Companies might emphasize or deemphasize some of these parameters on a case by case basis.

- Getting the job done - core skills and knowledge. Include communication (continuum of family, church, community and other institutions) that will allow you to adapt to any tectonic shifts in the economy and job market. - translated to work related productivity.
- Work habits and attitude.
- Likeability; compatibility with the other members of the team and stakeholders.
- Core values.
- Professional network or connections.
- Adhering to policy (discipline); adaptability to change.
- Network (support infrastructure).
- Asking salary or being affordable.
- Cost benefit ratio (training cost, compensation package: health insurance, pension included; agency fee, if any).
- References.
- Promotability.
- Health condition.
- Job retention.
- Flexibility.
- Availability.
- Other requirements of human resources or personnel (drivers license, professional license, security clearance, credit check, etc.).

Chapter 6: Guidelines for Keeping a Job

Summary: this chapter enumerates the general guidelines for keeping a job. Execute what applies to you in this chapter, or come up with something better.

Whatever job you have, dream job or otherwise, or, you are unemployed or underemployed, or you have yet to join the job market from high school or college, it will be in your best interest to meet the following minimal guidelines: (a) you are healthy; (b) be the best you could possibly be in that specialization; (c) be the most productive practitioner in that category, in terms of skills, knowledge, network and potential; (d) you are cost effective for employers to hire, or retain or contract with (it will not be in your interest to price yourself out of the market); (e) have a pleasant personality and have a compatible value-system with that of your employer(s) and stakeholders; (f) you are flexible; (g) you have other job alternatives on the side; (h) you are diversified and prepared for the "worst" of the worse (including but not limited to building savings for the rainy day); (i) you are up-to-date with the developments in your company, industry and community (do not be the last one to know that is something is going to happen that will negatively impact you); (j) you are close to your support infrastructure (family, friends and peers); and, (k) you adhere to the "cradle to grave" preparations as enumerated in Chapter 7 of this book.

If there are gaps in the 11 guidelines above, I recommend that you reevaluate your approach, priorities and compensate for the gaps one way or another, or come up with something better.

If you have been too comfortable for a long time without adequately preparing for the next cycle of peaks and valleys, you might find yourself ill equipped when circumstances abruptly change. It will be in your best interest to review and assess the possible implications to you and your family of the realities enumerated in Chapter 4: Current Economic Conditions and Expectations of this book.

Keep in mind that once your savings and buffers ran out, the tendency is to panic. Once you panic, you are no longer in the best of shape to make the right decisions. This is why you need to be close to you support infrastructure.

For job search resources, please refer to Appendix F of this book.

Make the most of what you have while implementing your job recovery strategy. If you do the right thing, whenever there is a down side, what usually follows is an upside - but only if you make the required preparations and investments. For reinforcement, please read and click through the links in Appendix C: Verses to Cheer You Up, Appendix D: Movies to Cheer You Up, and Appendix E: Music to Cheer You Up in this book, including listening to the music and watching the movies.

Chapter 7: "Cradle to Grave" Preparations

Summary: Any meaning system-wide recovery will require public and private sector partnership, seriously rethinking our approach, and a program no less than that of the "Marshall Plan". Execute what applies to you in this chapter, or come up with something better.

- For parents and guardians - be proficient in parenting, teaching and guiding the children and the next generation. There is much blaming the school system, the church and other institutions for the academic performance of our students, when in fact, the root causes of the problem is a combination of the following: parents working 2-3 jobs concurrently and not able to attend to the needs of their children, or a dysfunctional or irresponsible or misguided parenting and support system. Successful job search and survival start from home and at the earliest possible age. Though this is not the focus of this book - for our own sake, at some point, we should have a national dialogue on the culture and policies that have been breeding the following: (1) parents and guardians having less time and opportunities to be with their children because they need multiple jobs to survive and keep up; (2) measuring success quantitatively but not qualitatively; (3) if we keep this up, we would have irreversibly lose our heart, soul, the previous and next generations; and therefore, (4) creating a perfect storm for our downfall! Is this really what we aspire for and want? Please refer to 'Grandparents raising Grandchildren' in Chapter 4 of this book.
- For children and the youth - freedom and discipline are not mutually exclusive values. Respect your parents and authority - what goes around comes around, or what you plant today is what you will reap in the future. Be an informed, caring and responsible citizen. Study well and cultivate good habits and values. Stay away from trouble. Learn the lessons of the 2008 global financial meltdown, particularly the roles of greed and the catastrophic collapse of governance. Learn and master good governance for you will be the future. Read the rest of this book.
- For public officials and policy makers - our economic problems are man-made, self-inflicted - exacerbated by brutal demagoguery and self interests. Thanks to you and your peers, collectively we are playing into the hands of our enemies in creating a perfect storm that facilitates an implosion from within and diminished capabilities. Due to a catastrophic failure of governance - both

public and corporate - we find ourselves in a quagmire we are currently in, including the loss of millions of jobs, and which will take a long time to recover from. Don't you see the hand writing in the wall? What will it take for you and your peers to wake up and see what you have collectively done? For specifics, please refer to Chapter 4: Current Economic Conditions and Expectations of this book. **We need a Marshall plan to revive our national capabilities and confidence.**

- Citizens - exercise your voting rights! Elect and choose public officials and policy makers based on what they are capable of delivering, in being pragmatic, and not based on anachronistic ideologies. Select leaders who are capable of grasping, formulating, and executing policies that will move and uplift the economy and the country. Vote out those public officials and policy makers who have been engaging in endless demagoguery and rhetoric, and who have been clueless on the realities of our diminished financial capabilities and status that they themselves have created and exacerbated. Be vigilant against the machinations of political propaganda. Voting allows you to articulate your voice and influence policies on long-term job creation, school reform, tax reform, tort reform, pension reform, and other pertinent matters. Keep in mind that the "best practices and lessons learned" in this book and/or other books only make sense if there are jobs to be filled, and this is not going to be the case if we keep electing and supporting public officials and policy makers who keep mismanaging the economy and leading us into a catastrophic train wreck! For specifics, please refer to Chapter 4: Current Economic Conditions and Expectations of this book.

- Each person you bring to your team, either adds value or diminishes the value of the group. Reach out and recruit individuals with insight, multi-disciplinary experience and passion in uplifting the team.

- Invest in a **"sustained"** and **"agile"** lifelong learning across disciplines and boundaries. To optimize your job options - secure knowledge, skills and connections in white collar and blue collar professions. Diversify your knowledge, skills and network. Community colleges and adult schools are starting platforms for this. The ability to retool and adapt is key in today's fast-paced environment.

- Get yourself organized like other community groups with aggressive and agile infrastructure in systematically training and positioning for future jobs today. This could take the form of a cooperative.

- Learn and master other cultures and languages. As a starting point, review and consider Appendix G: Une Journée dans la vie d'un Imbécile: 8/26/2011 of this book.

- Volunteer in projects where people of endearing values participate or congregate; maintain contact with these people. Keep in mind that most people with endearing values might not be likeable from your perspective. There are relationships that you will need to nurture and protect at all costs (because they are worth it), and there are relationships that simply take space and time but do not add real value.

- Cultivate discipline, good working habits and ethics as early as possible. There are constant and numerous complains from employers suggest that a good number of young people today have limited attention span, text a lot times while working, and need to be praised all the time regardless of job performance.

- Analyze job and business requirements and trends before enrolling and investing time and resources; focus on growing industries. Preparing for, capturing and keeping a stable job is demanding and challenging process. Please refer to the Appendices A and B sections of this book for job statistics from the U.S. Department of Labor – Bureau of Labor Statistics and International Labor Organization. The strategy of blindly or haphazardly investing time and resources into a job or career (that may not exist at a later time or not bring in sufficient income or both) without doing your homework is referred to as "Feast and Famine" or the "Charge of the Light Brigade".

- Make a choice: a pain of regret (reactive strategy) or pain of hard work (proactive strategy). The younger you start, or the earlier you make the right decision, the better it is for you. If you delay the right decision, you will probably spend the rest of your life correcting and paying the price for what you should have done right the first time. Do not expect to harvest anything of substance if you have neither done your homework nor invested in the process.

To be effective in today's increasingly competitive market, job seekers will need to seriously consider at least 2 extremes, namely: being a paranoid, or living like a fruit fly - or something in between. For specifics, I refer you to:

- Only the Paranoid Survive: How to Exploit the Crisis Points That Challenge Every Company by Andrew Grove

  http://en.wikipedia.org/wiki/Andrew_Grove

- Live Like A Fruit Fly by Gabe Berman

  http://amaze-magazine.com/2011/08/live-like-a-fruit-fly-by-gabe-berman/

Chapter 8: Scenario - What to Do When You Are Laid off or About to Be Laid Off?

Summary: stay calm and execute what applies to you in this chapter, or come up with something better.

What to do:

- It is normal to feel shocked, even traumatized and paralyzed for a while. Be calm and manage the situation as one of those peaks and valleys that you successfully went through and overcame before. Remember, this happens to the best of us, and that you should manage the situation, instead of the situation managing you.

  For inspiration, sing your favorite songs, or engage people who could provide direction, or motivate, or make you feel better. Stay away from people who are cynical, or who will not add value to your cause. Read and click through the links in Appendix C: Verses to Cheer You Up, Appendix D: Movies to Cheer You Up, and Appendix E: Music to Cheer You Up in this book, including listening to the music and watching the movies.

- If available, negotiate a severance package with your employer's human resources or your reporting channel.
- If available, explore job transition, search and retraining programs provided by your employer, city, state and federal agencies.
- If you or covered family members have medical or dental conditions where your employer's HMO/TPO or Self-funded program is the payer, talk to your provider and payor right away and work out extended coverage and payment options. The human resources or personnel is usually the starting point for this process. You might also qualify for a COBRA program (http://www.dol.gov/ebsa/cobra.html.). Please do this right away because this is usually an expensive item.

  The following websites will also assist you in negotiating your healthcare bills:

  http://www. healthcarebluebook.com

http://www.nytimes.com/2009/03/14/health/14patient.html

http://magazine.angieslist.com/doctors/articles/negotiating-health-care-bills-a-growing-trend.aspx

http://frugalliving.about.com/od/beautyhealthcare/a/How-To-Negotiate-Your-Medical-Bills.htm

- Where appropriate and at the earliest possible moment, discuss the situation with your family members or support group or both, and develop a plan as a team. Do not be too proud or be a macho to open with people you trust and those who could provide direction and uplift you.
- Immediately reduce your expenses and commitments to the bare minimum. Review your financial and other obligations, and where appropriate, renegotiate the terms of payments. This includes but not limited to: mortgage, car payments, insurance, credit card payments, etc. Project your expenses in increments of 3 months up to 2-3 years into the future, or more. With the economic realities enumerated in Chapter 4, it will be very nasty and brutal for a long time. Make sure that that you review Chapter 4: Current Economic Conditions and Expectations, and Chapter 7: "Cradle to Grave" Preparations of this book. Consider the possibility that you might deplete your resources prior to landing an alternative source of income.
- Consider taking an interim job to maintain your buffer and while you are looking for a longer term solution.
- Consider being a volunteer while looking for a longer term solution.
- Protect your credit record. Keep in mind that most employers will check on your credit profile as part of the hiring process. You do not want to create a situation in the future where prospective employers wanted to hire you but your credit profile is standing in the way.
- Be physically and mentally active. Keep yourself sharp and keep practicing your skills. This is where the right support group will keep pushing or pulling you until the situation is stabilized.
- Develop a job recovery plan; and execute the plan as if there is no tomorrow. If you followed the guidelines in Chapters 6 and 7, you should have a starting point of recovering systematically. If you have not followed the guidelines these guidelines, either you

get started right way, or come up with something better. The worse thing you could do is to stay home, or do nothing, or be surrounded by the wrong people.. Review Appendix F: Job Search Resources of this book.

- Conduct a post-mortem of your career and personal life; rethink and regroup. There is an opportunity here to assess your career, personal life, priorities and where you are heading. I know lots of people where being laid off was a blessing in disguise, and what appeared to be a set back turned out to be the trigger for propelling them in a different direction where they blossomed and thrived and grew in ways that would not have been possible if they remained where they were.

Signs of possible lay-offs or termination:

- Hiring freeze
- Company or department is not meeting targets
- Office gossips
- Cuts in budget
- Company gets acquired or merged
- Company's stock price is down
- Company is moving to smaller facilities
- Lack of maintenance on equipment and services
- Efficiency experts are brought in
- Increased number of secret meetings
- Management instability
- Blame game escalates
- Job duties are marginalized
- Cuts in pay
- Direct reports are bypassing normal channels
- Not invited in meetings or not copied in emails
- Routine expenses are cut unexpectedly
- Key business activities dry up
- Company starts outsourcing internal projects
- Peers starting losing their jobs
- Increased security levels
- Supervisors are too busy to meet with their direct reports
- Job reassignment without a request for transfer

Chapter 9: Scenario – I will Stay Where I am

Summary: Depending on what stage you are at, there are times when a promotion is not desirable or limiting one's options.

Scenario - Mr. Walker lives a comfortable life and has Position A1 in a national company and had the opportunity to be promoted to the next levels, namely: Positions A2 and A3, respectively. Position A2 is paid an additional $5,000 per year plus the prestige that goes along with the position, and of course, from Position A2, the opportunity to be promoted to Position A3. After considerable thought, Mr. Walker declined the promotion.

Rightfully or wrongfully, Mr. Walker analyzed the situation and concluded the following. He is currently being paid $X gross per annum with benefits at Position A1. The promotion to Position A2 will be provide him with $X + $5000 gross per annum with benefits plus prestige. The next promotion to Position A3 will provide him with $X + $5000 + $5000 gross per annum with benefits plus more prestige. The average longevity for Position A1 is10+ years and there are approximately 2,000 equivalent jobs in the local market (which translates to an abundance of options); for Position A2, the average longevity is 3 years and there are approximately 200 positions in the local market (which translates to less options than that of Position A1); for Position A3, the average longevity is 2 years and there are approximately 20 positions in the local market (which translates to less options compared to those of Positions A1 and A2). At this stage of his life, Mr. Walker felt that he is happy where he is. As a matter of contingency, Mr. Walker follows guidelines in Chapters 6 and 7 of this book.

Chapter 10: Scenario – Retooling and Transitioning to Another Job

Summary: retooling and transitioning to another job require planning and investment of resources.

Scenario - Mr. Jones (50 years old) and Mrs., Jones (45 years old), husband and wife, both worked for Company BBB, a national healthcare company with headquarters in a fast-paced, highly congested and high-crime rate area. If they want to remain in their respective specializations, there are only 7 other companies nationwide which can use and afford their knowledge and skills, and these companies are either in a highly congested and high crime-rate areas, or in locations where they do not want relocating to. For less pay, Mr. Jones and Mrs. Jones wanted to settle down in a smaller community with decent space and remote from the pressures of major metropolitan areas. Issues: (1) If there is downsizing or the company merged or is taken over, both of them could lose their jobs within months of each other. (2) Their pay grades and skills are such that only the other 7 companies will be interested and could afford to hire them, and working for those other companies is not an option for them. (3) How do they transition from where they are currently, to where they want to be – which is to work in a smaller community setting?

Rather than wait for what might happen, while the economy is strong and their health being superb, for less pay, Mr. Jones started working for a smaller healthcare company which provides services that are highly in demand in smaller communities. In preparation for this move, he enrolled in a local community college and expanded and retooled his knowledge and skills. Two years later, Mrs. Jones followed working for another smaller but different company that has equivalent operations in smaller communities. The transition took 5 years for both Mr. Jones and Mrs. Jones. At the beginning of the 6th year, they have the option to work anywhere in the country in a small community setting.

Chapter 11: Scenario - What to do When You Are a Happy Camper?

Summary: Do your part in uplifting and empowering others.

Boy, you are a fortunate son of a gun!!! You are the envy of the world!!!

To you, I salute and respectfully recommend to:

- Keep developing and nurturing your gifts. Share your blessings, wisdom and experience with others. Lift and empower others, and in so doing, you further lift and empower yourself! Consider being a resource person as enumerated in Chapters 6 and 7 of this book. Please refer to the following (David Gregory of Meet The Press goes one-on-one to mentor a new friend):

  http://www.usaweekend.com/article/20110923/LIVING03/30
  9230012/David-Gregory-Meet-Press-goes-one-one-mentor-new-
  friend

- Call and say hello to a relative or friend or associate that you had a falling out with, and had not talked with for a long long time. Has it ever occurred to you that one of you might have overreacted, or said something inappropriate? Regardless of whether that is the case or not, that would neither be the first time nor the last time, right? Bury the hatchet and move on! Encourage others to do the same.
- Visit a church, or a temple, or a synagogue or a mosque. Engage your priest, or nun, or minister, or rabbi, or imam, or mentor, or mentees, or all of them.
- Visit or volunteer at a foster homes, orphanages, facilities for the disabled, free clinics, shelters, churches, temples, synagogues, mosques, and other institutions and programs that uplift and empower the less fortunate.
- Visit animal shelters. Plant trees. Recycle materials.
- Visit the airport or bus or train stations and observe departing passengers waving good bye to their loved ones, or arriving passengers embracing loves ones they have not seen for a while. This might prove to be a touching and endearing experience. Perhaps this is one way of revisiting your roots and earlier times when things were much simpler and you were more idealistic.

- Review <u>Appendix H: Expand Your Horizon</u> and the other appendices of this book.

Chapter 12: Summary

Summary: Preparing for, capturing and keeping a stable job is a demanding and challenging process. Long-term job stability requires a continuum of well planned, coordinated and executed policies, and a strong public and private sector partnership.

<u>Briefly:</u>

- At the youngest possible age, start acquiring skills, knowledge, habits and attitudes that are most valued in the industry and good for your health.
- Diversify your skills, knowledge and network.
- Network with the best people and groups that uplift and empower. Stay away from demagogues and people with attitude. Build and nurture a functional and sustainable family and support group that will be with you comes rain or shine.
- Cultivate and nurture good relationships with your peers, clients and stakeholders.
- Research the market, industry and job trends on an ongoing basis. Refer to <u>Appendix A: 2008 thru 2018 U.S. Job Projections</u>, and <u>Appendix B: International Unemployment Rates and Employment Indexes, Seasonally Adjusted</u>.
- Understand why some models are better than others and under what conditions, and incorporate the **"lessons learned and best practices"** into your repertoire of tools.
- Engage in a lifelong and sustained learning program. Engage and learn from other cultures; learn another language; travel to other countries. Learning, adapting and retooling is a journey, not a destination.
- Prepare for the worst, including building your savings for the rainy day.
- There are times when it is in your interest to take a pay cut rather losing a job.
- Make sure that you make time for self-development and quality time with people that are closest to you. Do not get caught in the inertia trap where the process manages you, instead of you managing the process. We all make choices in life that makes the world around us either better or worse; what we say and do have implications far beyond our borders and into future generations.
- Uplift and empower others.

- Exercise good citizenship, including but not limited to exercising your voting rights to elect knowledgeable and pragmatic public officials and policy makers. Be constantly reminded that it was us who elected them, and who mismanaged the economy and led us into a catastrophic global financial meltdown in 2008! For specifics and reinforcement, review Chapter 4: Current Economic Conditions and Expectations, and Chapter 7: "Cradle to Grave" Preparations. The best **"practices and lessons learned"** in this book and/or other books only make sense if there are jobs to be filled, and this is not going to be the case if we keep electing and supporting public officials and policy makers who are vent on "destructive" defederalization and the dismemberment of this great country in the direction of the European Union with 17 different and incompatible policies - which is hardly a model for responding to a man-made and man-exacerbated quagmire that we are currently in!

  "The value of the whole is much more than the value of its individual components" and the capacity to work together despite differences are two of the guiding principles that differentiated us from the rest of the world and catapulted this country to be a leader in the 20th century. We need to select leaders who are capable to restoring and operating within these core values into the 21st century.

I recommend that you take the time go through the verses and internet links in the Appendix sections of this book, including listening to the music and watching the movies. Within the context of this book, collectively - these are structured to provide you with a different perspective and experience utilizing text and various multi-media tools. If you wish to receive an updated list of the hyperlinks in this book, please send an email message to jobsurvival-subscribe@yahoogroups.com, or JobSurvival2012.Beyond@gmail.com.

I am hoping that you find something of value to you in this book. I thank you for your patience and time. The author can be reached via: JobSurvival2012.Beyond@gmail.com.

Appendix A: 2008 thru 2018 U.S. Job Projections

Summary: These are job projections in the U.S. between 2008 thru 2018.

U.S. Department of Labor – Bureau of Labor Statistics

http://www.bls.gov

BLS: Table 1.4 – Occupations with the largest job growth, 2008 and projected 2018

Table 1.4 Occupations with the largest job growth, 2008 and projected 2018
(Numbers in thousands)

2008 National Employment Matrix title and code		Major occupational group	Employment 2008	Employment 2018	Change, 2008-18 Number	Change, 2008-18 Percent	Median Annual wage quartile, 2008	Most significant source of postsecondary education or training
Registered nurses	29-1111	Professional and related	2,618.7	3,200.2	581.5	22.20	VH	Associate degree
Home health aides	31-1011	Service	921.7	1,382.6	460.9	50.01	VL	Short-term on-the-job training
Customer service representatives	43-4051	Office and administrative support	2,252.4	2,651.9	399.5	17.74	L	Moderate-term on-the-job training
Combined food preparation and serving workers, including fast food	35-3021	Service	2,701.7	3,096.0	394.3	14.59	VL	Short-term on-the-job training
Personal and home care aides	39-9021	Service	817.2	1,193.0	375.8	45.99	VL	Short-term on-the-job training
Retail salespersons	41-2031	Sales and related	4,489.2	4,863.9	374.7	8.35	VL	Short-term on-the-job training
Office clerks, general	43-9061	Office and administrative support	3,024.4	3,383.1	358.7	11.86	L	Short-term on-the-job training
Accountants and auditors	13-2011	Management, business, and financial	1,290.6	1,570.0	279.4	21.65	VH	Bachelor's degree
Nursing aides, orderlies, and attendants	31-1012	Service	1,469.8	1,745.8	276.0	18.76	L	Postsecondary vocational award
Postsecondary teachers	25-1000	Professional and related	1,699.2	1,956.1	256.9	15.12	VH	Doctoral degree
Construction laborers	47-2061	Construction and extraction	1,248.7	1,504.6	255.9	20.49	L	Moderate-term on-the-job training
Elementary school teachers, except special education	25-2021	Professional and related	1,549.5	1,793.7	244.2	13.76	H	Bachelor's degree
Truck drivers, heavy and tractor-trailer	53-3032	Transportation and material moving	1,798.4	2,031.3	232.9	12.95	H	Short-term on-the-job training
Landscaping and groundskeeping workers	37-3011	Service	1,205.8	1,422.9	217.1	18.00	L	Short-term on-the-job training
Bookkeeping, accounting, and auditing clerks	43-3031	Office and administrative support	2,063.8	2,276.2	212.4	10.29	H	Moderate-term on-the-job training
Executive secretaries and administrative assistants	43-6011	Office and administrative support	1,594.4	1,798.8	204.4	12.82	H	Work experience in a related occupation
Management analysts	13-1111	Management, business, and financial	746.9	925.2	178.3	23.87	VH	Bachelor's or higher degree, plus work experience
Computer software engineers, applications	15-1031	Professional and related	514.8	689.9	175.1	34.01	VH	Bachelor's degree
Receptionists and information clerks	43-4171	Office and administrative support	1,139.2	1,312.1	172.9	15.18	L	Short-term on-the-job training
Carpenters	47-2031	Construction and extraction	1,284.9	1,450.3	165.4	12.87	H	Long-term on-the-job training
Medical assistants	31-9092	Service	483.6	647.5	163.9	33.90	L	Moderate-term on-the-job training
First-line supervisors/managers of office and administrative support workers	43-1011	Office and administrative support	1,457.2	1,617.5	160.3	11.00	H	Work experience in a related occupation
Network systems and data communications analysts	15-1081	Professional and related	292.0	447.8	155.8	53.36	VH	Bachelor's degree
Licensed practical and licensed vocational nurses	29-2061	Professional and related	753.6	909.2	155.6	20.65	H	Postsecondary vocational award
Security guards	33-9032	Service	1,076.6	1,229.1	152.5	14.16	L	Short-term on-the-job training
Waiters and waitresses	35-3031	Service	2,381.6	2,533.3	151.6	6.37	VL	Short-term on-the-job training
Maintenance and repair workers, general	49-9042	Installation, maintenance, and repair	1,361.3	1,509.2	147.9	16.86	H	Moderate-term on-the-job training
Physicians and surgeons	29-1060	Professional and related	661.4	805.5	144.1	21.79	VH	First professional degree
Child care workers	39-9011	Service	1,301.9	1,443.9	142.1	16.91	VL	Short-term on-the-job training
Teacher assistants	25-9041	Professional and related	1,312.7	1,447.6	134.9	10.28	L	Short-term on-the-job training

Source: Employment Projections Program, U.S. Department of Labor, U.S. Bureau of Labor Statistics

BLS: Chart 3 – Percent of Labor Force by Age Group

Chart 3. **Percent of labor force, by age group**

Percent
of
labor force

■ 2008
□ 2018 (projected)

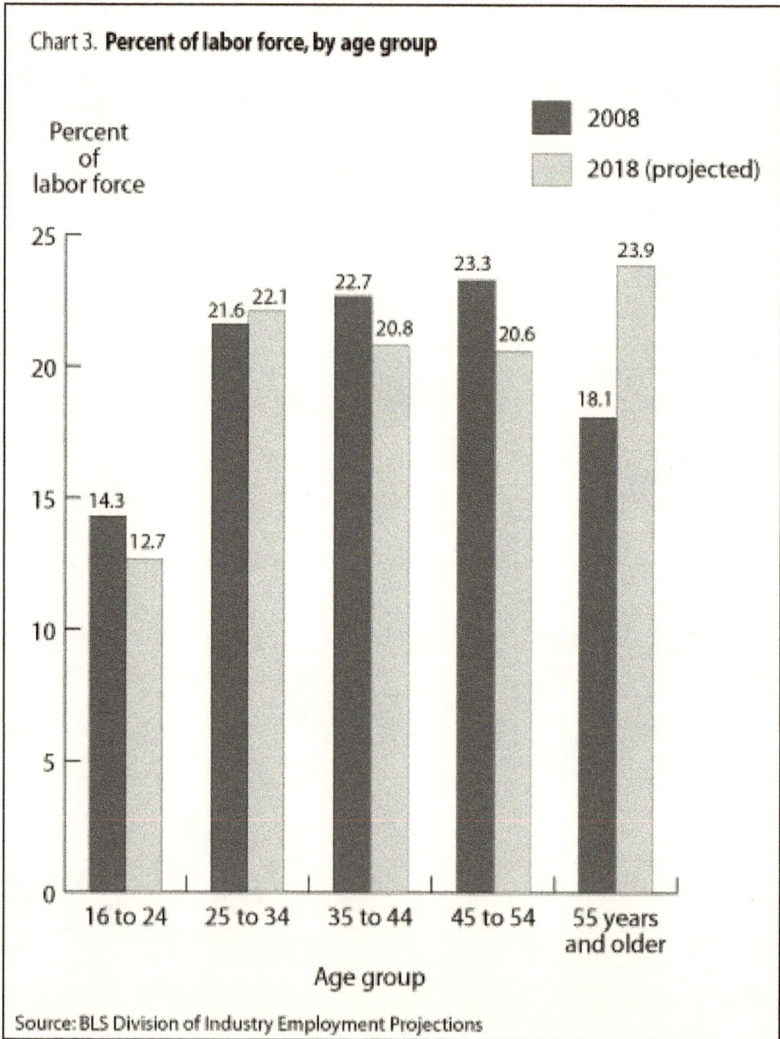

Source: BLS Division of Industry Employment Projections

The share of the youth labor force, workers aged 16 to 24, is expected to decrease from 14.3 percent in 2008 to 12.7 percent by 2018. The primary working-age group, those between 25 and 54 years old, is projected to decline from 67.7 percent of the labor force in 2008 to 63.5 percent by 2018. Workers aged 55 years and older, by contrast, are anticipated to leap from 18.1 percent to 23.9 percent of the labor force during the same period (Chart 3).

BLS: Chart 5 – Numeric change in wage and salary employment in service-providing industries, 2008-2018 (projected)

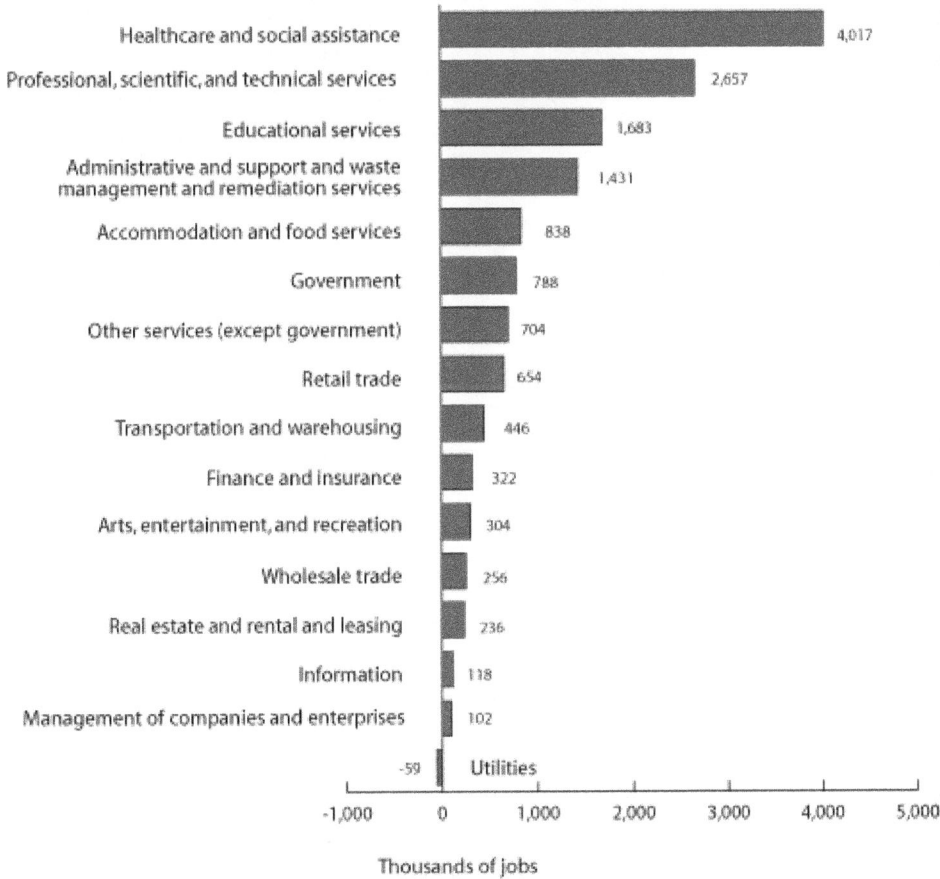

Chart 5. **Numeric change in wage and salary employment in service-providing industries, 2008–18 (projected)**

Industry	Thousands of jobs
Healthcare and social assistance	4,017
Professional, scientific, and technical services	2,657
Educational services	1,683
Administrative and support and waste management and remediation services	1,431
Accommodation and food services	838
Government	788
Other services (except government)	704
Retail trade	654
Transportation and warehousing	446
Finance and insurance	322
Arts, entertainment, and recreation	304
Wholesale trade	256
Real estate and rental and leasing	236
Information	118
Management of companies and enterprises	102
Utilities	-59

Thousands of jobs

Source: BLS National Employment Matrix

Service-providing industries. The shift in the U.S. economy away from goods-producing in favor of service-providing is expected to continue. Service-providing industries are anticipated to generate approximately 14.5 million new wage and salary jobs. As with goods-producing industries, growth among service-providing industries will vary (Chart 5).

Educational services. Employment in public and private educational services is anticipated to grow by 12 percent, adding about 1.7 million new jobs through 2018. Rising student enrollments at all levels of education will create demand for educational services.

Healthcare and social assistance. About 26 percent of all new jobs created in the U.S. economy will be in the healthcare and social assistance industry. This industry—which includes public and private hospitals, nursing and residential care facilities, and individual and family services—is expected to grow by 24 percent, or 4 million new jobs. Employment growth will be driven by an aging population and longer life expectancies.

Arts, entertainment, and recreation. The arts, entertainment, and recreation industry is expected to grow by 15 percent by 2018. Most of the growth will be in the amusement, gambling, and recreation sector. Job growth will stem from public participation in arts, entertainment, and recreation activities—reflecting increasing incomes, leisure time, and awareness of the health benefits of physical fitness.

Accommodation and food services. Employment in accommodation and food services is expected to grow by 7 percent, adding about 838,200 new jobs through 2018. Job growth will be concentrated in food services and drinking places, reflecting an increase in the population and the convenience of many new food establishments.

Other services (except government and private households). Employment is expected to grow by 13 percent in other services. Personal care services comprise the fastest growing industry in this sector, at 32 percent. This industry includes barbers, salons, and spas, which have experienced growing demand as individuals increasingly are seeking to improve their personal appearance.

Government. Between 2008 and 2018, government employment, excluding employment in public education and hospitals, is expected to increase by 7 percent. Growth in government employment will be fueled by expanding demand for public safety services and assistance provided to the elderly, but dampened by budgetary constraints and the outsourcing of government jobs to the private sector. State and local governments, excluding education and hospitals, are anticipated to grow by 8 percent as a result of the continued shift of responsibilities from the Federal Government to State and local governments. Federal Government employment, including the Postal Service, is expected to increase by 3 percent.

BLS: Chart 6 – Percent change in total employment, by major occupational group, 2008-2018 (projected)

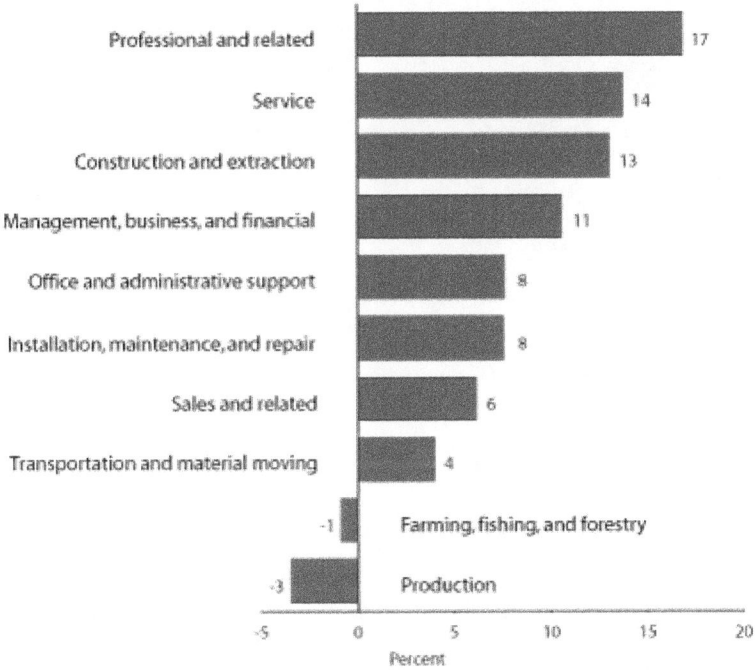

Chart 6. **Percent change in total employment, by major occupational group, 2008–18 (projected)**

Occupational group	Percent
Professional and related	17
Service	14
Construction and extraction	13
Management, business, and financial	11
Office and administrative support	8
Installation, maintenance, and repair	8
Sales and related	6
Transportation and material moving	4
Farming, fishing, and forestry	-1
Production	-3

Percent

Source: BLS National Employment Matrix

Employment change by occupation

(A) Back to Top

Industry growth or decline will affect demand for occupations. However, job growth is projected to vary among major occupational groups (Chart 6).

BLS: Table 1 – Occupations with the fastest growth

Table 1. Occupations with the fastest growth

Occupations	Percent change	Number of new jobs (in thousands)	Wages (May 2008 median)	Education/training category
Biomedical engineers	72	11.6	$ 77,400	Bachelor's degree
Network systems and data communications analysts	53	155.8	71,100	Bachelor's degree
Home health aides	50	460.9	20,460	Short-term on-the-job training
Personal and home care aides	46	375.8	19,180	Short-term on-the-job training
Financial examiners	41	11.1	70,930	Bachelor's degree
Medical scientists, except epidemiologists	40	44.2	72,590	Doctoral degree
Physician assistants	39	29.2	81,230	Master's degree
Skin care specialists	38	14.7	28,730	Postsecondary vocational award
Biochemists and biophysicists	37	8.7	82,840	Doctoral degree
Athletic trainers	37	6.0	39,640	Bachelor's degree
Physical therapist aides	36	16.7	23,760	Short-term on-the-job training
Dental hygienists	36	62.9	66,570	Associate degree
Veterinary technologists and technicians	36	28.5	28,900	Associate degree
Dental assistants	36	105.6	32,380	Moderate-term on-the-job training
Computer software engineers, applications	34	175.1	85,430	Bachelor's degree
Medical assistants	34	163.9	28,300	Moderate-term on-the-job training
Physical therapist assistants	33	21.2	46,140	Associate degree
Veterinarians	33	19.7	79,050	First professional degree
Self-enrichment education teachers	32	81.3	35,720	Work experience in a related occupation
Compliance officers, except agriculture, construction, health and safety, and transportation	31	80.8	48,890	Long-term on-the-job training

SOURCE: BLS Occupational Employment Statistics and Division of Occupational Outlook

Two of the fastest growing detailed occupations are in the computer specialist occupational group. Network systems and data communications analysts are projected to be the second-fastest-growing occupation in the economy. Demand for these workers will increase as organizations continue to upgrade their information technology capacity and incorporate the newest technologies. The growing reliance on wireless networks will result in a need for more network systems and data communications analysts as well. Computer applications software engineers also are expected to grow rapidly from 2008 to 2018. Expanding Internet technologies have spurred demand for these workers, who can develop Internet, intranet, and Web applications.

Developments from biotechnology research will continue to be used to create new medical technologies, treatments, and pharmaceuticals. As a result, demand for medical scientists and for biochemists and biophysicists will increase. However, although employment of biochemists and biophysicists is projected to grow rapidly, this corresponds to only 8,700 new jobs over the projection period. Increased medical research and demand for new medical technologies also will affect biomedical engineers. The aging of the population and a growing focus on health issues will drive demand for better medical devices and equipment designed by these workers. In fact, biomedical engineers are projected to be the fastest growing occupation in the economy. However, because of its small size, the occupation is projected to add only about 11,600 jobs.

Increasing financial regulations will spur employment growth both of financial examiners and of compliance officers, except agriculture, construction, health and safety, and transportation.

Self-enrichment teachers and skin care specialists will experience growth as consumers become more concerned with self-improvement. Self-enrichment teachers are growing rapidly as more individuals seek additional training to make themselves more appealing to prospective employers. Skin care specialists will experience growth as consumers increasingly care about their personal appearance.

Of the 20 fastest growing occupations, 12 are in the associate degree or higher category. Of the remaining 8, 6 are in an on-the-job training category, 1 is in the work experience in a related occupation category, and 1 is in the postsecondary vocational degree category. Eleven of these occupations earn at least $10,000 more than the National annual median wage, which was $32,390 as of May 2008. In fact, 9 of the occupations earned at least twice the National median in May 2008.

Occupations with the largest numerical growth. The 20 occupations listed in table 2 are projected to account for more than one-third of all new jobs—5.8 million combined—over the 2008-18 period. The occupations with the largest numerical increases cover a wider range of occupational categories than do those occupations with the fastest growth rates. Health occupations will account for some of these increases in employment, as will occupations in education, sales, and food service. Office and administrative support services occupations are expected to grow by 1.3 million jobs, accounting for about one-fifth of the job growth among the 20 occupations with the largest growth. Many of the occupations listed in the table are very large and will create more new jobs than occupations with high growth rates. Only 3 out of the 20 fastest growing occupations—home health aides, personal and home care aides, and computer software application engineers—also are projected to be among the 20 occupations with the largest numerical increases in employment.

BLS: Table 2 – Occupations with the largest numerical growth

Table 2. Occupations with the largest numerical growth

Occupations	Number of new jobs (in thousands)	Percent change	Wages (May 2008 median)	Education/training category
Registered nurses	581.5	22	$ 62,450	Associate degree
Home health aides	460.9	50	20,460	Short-term on-the-job training
Customer service representatives	399.5	18	29,860	Moderate-term on-the-job training
Combined food preparation and serving workers, including fast food	394.3	15	16,430	Short-term on-the-job training
Personal and home care aides	375.8	46	19,180	Short-term on-the-job training
Retail salespersons	374.7	8	20,510	Short-term on-the-job training
Office clerks, general	358.7	12	25,320	Short-term on-the-job training
Accountants and auditors	279.4	22	59,430	Bachelor's degree
Nursing aides, orderlies, and attendants	276.0	19	23,850	Postsecondary vocational award
Postsecondary teachers	256.9	15	58,830	Doctoral degree
Construction laborers	255.9	20	28,520	Moderate-term on-the-job training
Elementary school teachers, except special education	244.2	16	49,330	Bachelor's degree
Truck drivers, heavy and tractor-trailer	232.9	13	37,270	Short-term on-the-job training
Landscaping and groundskeeping workers	217.1	18	23,150	Short-term on-the-job training
Bookkeeping, accounting, and auditing clerks	212.4	10	32,510	Moderate-term on-the-job training
Executive secretaries and administrative assistants	204.4	13	40,030	Work experience in a related occupation
Management analysts	178.3	24	73,570	Bachelor's or higher degree, plus work experience
Computer software engineers, applications	175.1	34	85,430	Bachelor's degree
Receptionists and information clerks	172.9	15	24,550	Short-term on-the-job training
Carpenters	165.4	13	38,940	Long-term on-the-job training

SOURCE: BLS Occupational Employment Statistics and Division of Occupational Outlook

The education or training categories and wages of the occupations with the largest numbers of new jobs are significantly different than those of the fastest growing occupations. Twelve of these occupations are in an on-the-job training category, and just 7 are in a category that indicates any postsecondary education. Ten of the 20 occupations with the largest numbers of new jobs earned less than the National median wage in May 2008.

Occupations with the fastest decline. Declining occupational employment stems from falling industry employment, technological advances, changes in business practices, and other factors. For example, technological developments and the continued movement of textile production abroad are expected to contribute to a decline of 71,500 sewing machine operators over the projection period (table 3). Fifteen of the 20 occupations with the largest numerical decreases are either production occupations or office and administrative support occupations, both of which are adversely affected by increasing plant and factory automation or the implementation of office technology, reducing the need for workers in those occupations. The difference between the office and administrative support occupations that are expected to experience the largest declines and those which are expected to see the largest increases is the extent to which job functions can be easily automated or performed by other workers. For instance, the duties of executive secretaries and administrative assistants involve a great deal of personal interaction that cannot be automated, whereas the duties of file clerks—adding, locating, and removing business records—can be automated or performed by other workers.

BLS: Table 3 – Occupations with the fastest decline

Table 3. Occupations with the fastest decline

Occupation	Percent change	Number of jobs lost (in thousands)	Wages (May 2008 median)	Education/training category
Textile bleaching and dyeing machine operators and tenders	-45	-7.2	$ 23,680	Moderate-term on-the-job training
Textile winding, twisting, and drawing out machine setters, operators, and tenders	-41	-14.2	23,970	Moderate-term on-the-job training
Textile knitting and weaving machine setters, operators, and tenders	-39	-11.5	25,400	Long-term on-the-job training
Shoe machine operators and tenders	-35	-1.7	25,090	Moderate-term on-the-job training
Extruding and forming machine setters, operators, and tenders, synthetic and glass fibers	-34	-4.8	31,160	Moderate-term on-the-job training
Sewing machine operators	-34	-71.5	19,870	Moderate-term on-the-job training
Semiconductor processors	-32	-10.0	32,230	Postsecondary vocational award
Textile cutting machine setters, operators, and tenders	-31	-6.0	22,620	Moderate-term on-the-job training
Postal Service mail sorters, processors, and processing machine operators	-30	-54.5	50,020	Short-term on-the-job training
Fabric menders, except garment	-30	-0.3	28,470	Moderate-term on-the-job training
Wellhead pumpers	-28	-5.3	37,860	Moderate-term on-the-job training
Fabric and apparel patternmakers	-27	-2.2	37,760	Long-term on-the-job training
Drilling and boring machine tool setters, operators, and tenders, metal and plastic	-27	-8.9	30,850	Moderate-term on-the-job training
Lathe and turning machine tool setters, operators, and tenders, metal and plastic	-27	-14.9	32,940	Moderate-term on-the-job training
Order clerks	-26	-64.2	27,990	Short-term on-the-job training
Coil winders, tapers, and finishers	-25	-5.6	27,730	Short-term on-the-job training
Photographic processing machine operators	-24	-12.5	20,360	Short-term on-the-job training
File clerks	-23	-49.6	23,800	Short-term on-the-job training
Derrick operators, oil and gas	-23	-5.8	41,920	Moderate-term on-the-job training

BLS: Chart 7 – Percent change in employment, by education or training category, 2008-2018 (projected)

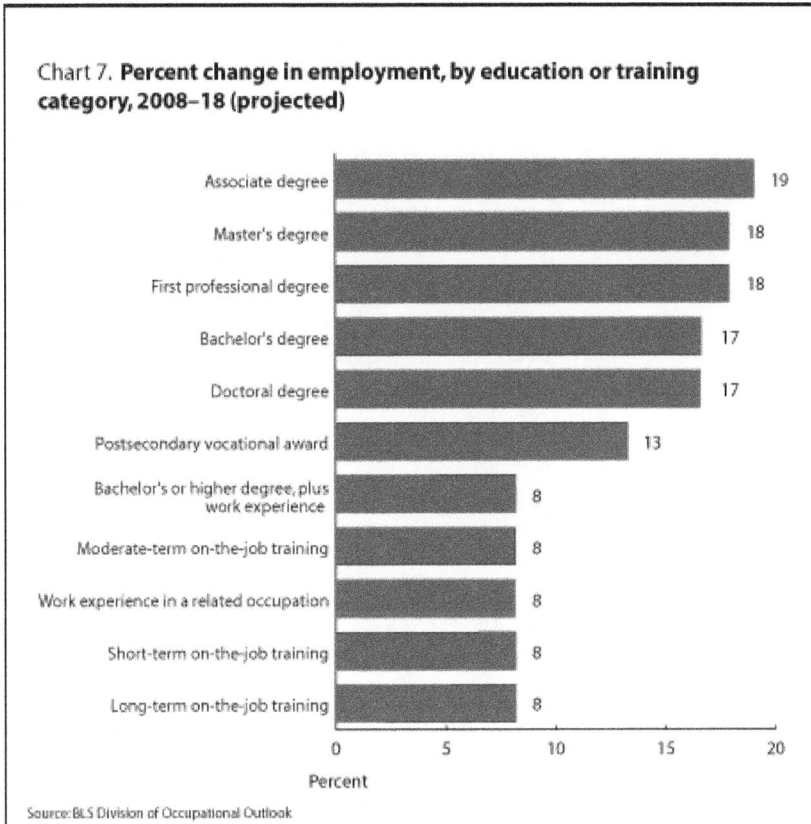

Chart 7. **Percent change in employment, by education or training category, 2008–18 (projected)**

Education or training category	Percent
Associate degree	19
Master's degree	18
First professional degree	18
Bachelor's degree	17
Doctoral degree	17
Postsecondary vocational award	13
Bachelor's or higher degree, plus work experience	8
Moderate-term on-the-job training	8
Work experience in a related occupation	8
Short-term on-the-job training	8
Long-term on-the-job training	8

Percent

Source: BLS Division of Occupational Outlook

Employment change by education and training category   (▲) Back to Top

Education and training categories for each occupation are determined by the most significant source of education and training obtained by workers in that occupation. Growth for each education and training category is calculated by adding the growth across all occupations in the category. As a result, there is some variation in the growth rates between categories.

In general, occupations in a category with some postsecondary education are expected to experience higher rates of growth than those in an on-the-job training category. Occupations in the associate degree category are projected to grow the fastest, at about 19 percent. In addition, occupations in the master's and first professional degree categories are anticipated to grow by about 18 percent each, and occupations in the bachelor's and doctoral degree categories are expected to grow by about 17 percent each. However, occupations in the on-the-job training categories are expected to grow by 8 percent each (Chart 7).

BLS: Chart 8 – Number of jobs due to growth and replacement needs, by major occupational group, 2008-2018 (projected)

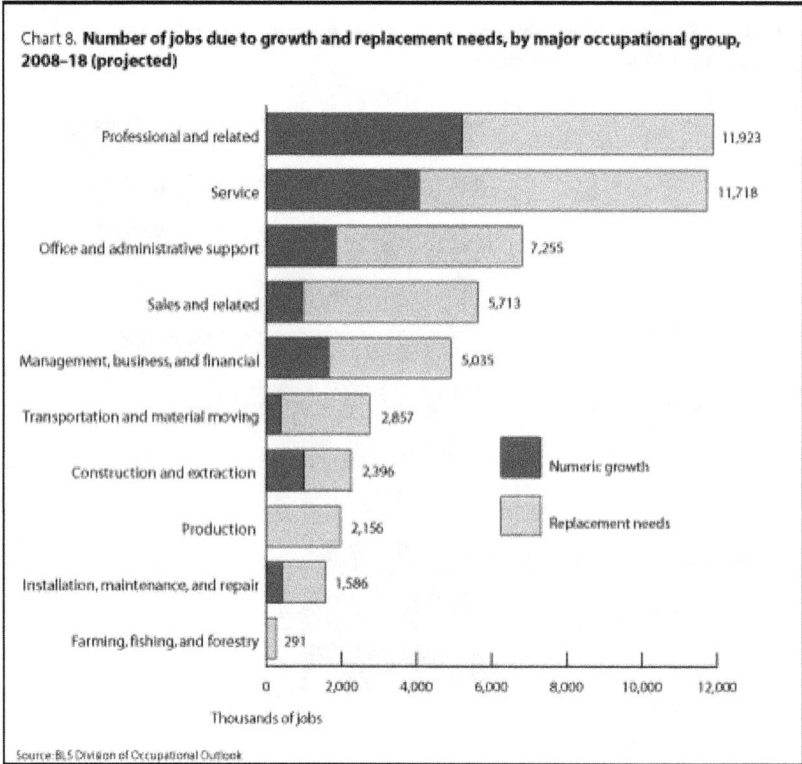

Chart 8. **Number of jobs due to growth and replacement needs, by major occupational group, 2008–18 (projected)**

Occupational group	Total (thousands)
Professional and related	11,923
Service	11,718
Office and administrative support	7,255
Sales and related	5,713
Management, business, and financial	5,035
Transportation and material moving	2,857
Construction and extraction	2,396
Production	2,156
Installation, maintenance, and repair	1,586
Farming, fishing, and forestry	291

Legend: ■ Numeric growth   □ Replacement needs

Thousands of jobs (x-axis: 0, 2,000, 4,000, 6,000, 8,000, 10,000, 12,000)

Source: BLS Division of Occupational Outlook

Classification of occupations by most significant source of education or training
Postsecondary awards

First professional degree. Completion of the degree usually requires at least 3 years of full-time academic study beyond a bachelor's degree. Examples are lawyers; and physicians and surgeons.

Doctoral degree. Completion of a Ph.D. or other doctoral degree usually requires at least 3 years of full-time academic study beyond a bachelor's degree. Examples are postsecondary teachers; and medical scientists, except epidemiologists.

Master's degree. Completion of the degree usually requires 1 or 2 years of full-time academic study beyond a bachelor's degree. Examples are educational, vocational, and school counselors; and clergy.

Bachelor's or higher degree, plus work experience. Most occupations in this category are management occupations. All require experience in a related nonmanagement position for which a bachelor's or higher degree is usually required. Examples are general and operations managers; and judges, magistrate judges, and magistrates.

Bachelor's degree. Completion of the degree generally requires at least 4 years, but not more than 5 years, of full-time academic study. Examples are accountants and auditors; and elementary school teachers, except special education.

Associate degree. Completion of the degree usually requires at least 2 years of full-time academic study. Examples are paralegals and legal assistants; and medical records and health information technicians.

Postsecondary vocational award. Some programs last only a few weeks, others more than a year. Programs lead to a certificate or other award, but not a degree. Examples are nursing aides, orderlies, and attendants; and hairdressers, hairstylists, and cosmetologists.

Work-related training

Work experience in a related occupation. Most of the occupations in this category are first-line supervisors or managers of service, sales and related, production, or other occupations; or are management occupations.

Long-term on-the-job training. Occupations in this category generally require more than 12 months of on-the-job training or combined work experience and formal classroom instruction for workers to develop the skills necessary to be fully qualified in the occupation. These occupations include formal and informal apprenticeships that may last up to 5 years. Long-term on-the-job training also includes intensive occupation-specific, employer-sponsored programs that workers must complete. Among such programs are those conducted by fire and police academies and by schools for air traffic controllers and flight attendants. In other occupations—insurance sales and securities sales, for example—trainees take formal courses, often provided on the jobsite, to prepare for the required licensing exams. Individuals undergoing training generally are considered to be employed in the occupation. Also included in this category is the development of a natural ability—such as that possessed by musicians, athletes, actors, and other entertainers—that must be cultivated over several years, frequently in a non-work setting.

Moderate-term on-the-job training. In this category of occupations, the skills needed to be fully qualified in the occupation can be acquired during 1 to 12 months of combined on-the-job experience and informal training. Examples are truckdrivers, heavy and tractor-trailer; and secretaries, except legal, medical, and executive.

Short-term on-the-job training. In occupations in this category, the skills needed to be fully qualified in the occupation can be acquired during a short demonstration of job duties or during 1 month or less of on-the-job experience or instruction. Examples of these occupations are retail salespersons; and waiters and waitresses.

Total job openings (▲) Back to Top

Job openings stem from both employment growth and replacement needs (Chart 8). Replacement needs arise as workers leave occupations. Some transfer to other occupations, while others retire, return to school, or quit to assume household responsibilities. Replacement needs are projected to account for 67 percent of the approximately 50.9 million job openings between 2008 and 2018. Thus, even occupations that are projected to experience slower-than-average growth or to decline in employment still may offer many job openings.

Professional and related occupations are projected to have the largest number of total job openings, 11.9 million, and 56 percent of those will be due to replacement needs. Replacement needs generally are greatest in the largest occupations and in those with relatively low pay or limited training requirements. As a result, service occupations are projected to have the greatest number of job openings due to replacements, about 7.6 million.

Office automation will significantly affect many individual office and administrative support occupations. Although these occupations are projected to grow about as fast as average, some are projected to decline rapidly. Office and administrative support occupations are expected to create 7.3 million total job openings from 2008 to 2018, ranking third behind professional and related occupations and service occupations.

Farming, fishing, and forestry occupations and production occupations should offer job opportunities despite overall declines in employment. These occupations will lose 9,100 and 349,200 jobs, respectively, but are expected to provide more than 2.4 million total job openings. Job openings will be due solely to the replacement needs of a workforce characterized by high levels of retirement and job turnover.

Classification of occupations by most significant source of education or training
Postsecondary awards

First professional degree. Completion of the degree usually requires at least 3 years of full-time academic study beyond a bachelor's degree. Examples are lawyers; and physicians and surgeons.

Doctoral degree. Completion of a Ph.D. or other doctoral degree usually requires at least 3 years of full-time academic study beyond a bachelor's degree. Examples are postsecondary teachers; and medical scientists, except epidemiologists.

Master's degree. Completion of the degree usually requires 1 or 2 years of full-time academic study beyond a bachelor's degree. Examples are educational, vocational, and school counselors; and clergy.

Bachelor's or higher degree, plus work experience. Most occupations in this category are management occupations. All require experience in a related nonmanagement position for which a bachelor's or higher degree is usually required. Examples are general and operations managers; and judges, magistrate judges, and magistrates.

Bachelor's degree. Completion of the degree generally requires at least 4 years, but not more than 5 years, of full-time academic study. Examples are accountants and auditors; and elementary school teachers, except special education.

Associate degree. Completion of the degree usually requires at least 2 years of full-time academic study. Examples are paralegals and legal assistants; and medical records and health information technicians.

Postsecondary vocational award. Some programs last only a few weeks, others more than a year. Programs lead to a certificate or other award, but not a degree. Examples are nursing aides, orderlies, and attendants; and hairdressers, hairstylists, and cosmetologists.

Work-related training

Work experience in a related occupation. Most of the occupations in this category are first-line supervisors or managers of service, sales and related, production, or other occupations; or are management occupations.

Long-term on-the-job training. Occupations in this category generally require more than 12 months of on-the-job training or combined work experience and formal classroom instruction for workers to develop the skills necessary to be fully qualified in the occupation. These occupations include formal and informal apprenticeships that may last up to 5 years. Long-term on-the-job training also includes intensive occupation-specific, employer-sponsored programs that workers must complete. Among such programs are those conducted by fire and police academies and by schools for air traffic controllers and flight attendants. In other occupations—insurance sales and securities sales, for example—trainees take formal courses, often provided on the jobsite, to prepare for the required licensing exams. Individuals undergoing training generally are considered to be employed in the occupation. Also included in this category is the development of a natural ability—such as that possessed by musicians, athletes, actors, and other entertainers—that must be cultivated over several years, frequently in a non-work setting.

Moderate-term on-the-job training. In this category of occupations, the skills needed to be fully qualified in the occupation can be acquired during 1 to 12 months of combined on-the-job experience and informal training. Examples are truckdrivers, heavy and tractor-trailer; and secretaries, except legal, medical, and executive.

Short-term on-the-job training. In occupations in this category, the skills needed to be fully qualified in the occupation can be acquired during a short demonstration of job duties or during 1 month or less of on-the-job experience or instruction. Examples of these occupations are retail salespersons; and waiters and waitresses.

BLS: Current Unemployment Rates for States and Historical Highs/Lows

Local Area Unemployment Statistics

Current Unemployment Rates for States and Historical Highs/Lows

Current Unemployment Rates for States and Historical Highs/Lows
Seasonally Adjusted

State	Aug. 2011[p] Rate	Historical High Date	Rate	Historical Low Date	Rate
Alabama	9.9	Dec. 1982	14.3	June 2007	3.3
Alaska	7.7	June 1986	11.5	Apr. 2007	5.9
Arizona	9.3	Jan. 1983	11.6	July 2007	3.6
Arkansas	8.3	July 1983	10.1	Nov. 2000	4.0
California	12.1	Dec. 2010	12.5	Jan. 2001	4.7
Colorado	8.5	Feb. 2011	9.3	Jan. 2001	2.6
Connecticut	9.0	Jan. 1976	9.4	Oct. 2000	2.1
Delaware	8.1	Dec. 1976	9.3	Feb. 1989	2.8
District of Columbia	11.1	Feb. 1983	11.6	May 1989	4.8
Florida	10.7	Dec. 2010	12.0	Aug. 2006	3.3
Georgia	10.2	Dec. 2010	10.4	Dec. 2000	3.3
Hawaii	6.2	Jan. 1976	9.9	Dec. 2006	2.3
Idaho	9.2	Mar. 2011	9.7	May 2007	2.7
Illinois	9.9	Feb. 1983	12.9	Feb. 1999	4.2
Indiana	8.7	Jan. 1983	12.7	Apr. 1999	2.6
Iowa	6.1	Mar. 1983	8.6	Oct. 1999	2.5
Kansas	6.7	Aug. 2009	7.6	Apr. 1979	3.0
Kentucky	9.5	Jan. 1983	12.0	June 2000	4.1
Louisiana	7.2	Nov. 1986	12.8	Sept. 2007	3.6
Maine	7.6	Jan. 1977	9.0	Jan. 2001	3.1
Maryland	7.3	Nov. 1982	8.4	Feb. 2000	3.4
Massachusetts	7.4	Jan. 1976	11.1	Oct. 2000	2.6
Michigan	11.2	Dec. 1982	16.8	Mar. 2000	3.3
Minnesota	7.2	Dec. 1982	9.1	Mar. 1999	2.5
Mississippi	10.3	Apr. 1983	13.5	Apr. 2001	4.9
Missouri	8.8	Feb. 1983	10.6	Jan. 2000	2.8
Montana	7.6	Mar. 1983	8.8	Mar. 2007	3.1
Nebraska	4.2	Feb. 1983	6.7	Feb. 1998	2.2
Nevada	13.4	Dec. 2010	14.9	Apr. 2000	3.8
New Hampshire	5.3	Sept. 1992	7.6	May 1987	2.1
New Jersey	9.4	Dec. 1976	10.7	July 2000	3.6
New Mexico	6.8	Mar. 1983	10.0	Nov. 2007	3.4
New York	8.0	Nov. 1976	10.3	Apr. 1988	4.0
North Carolina	10.4	Feb. 2010	11.4	Mar. 1999	3.1
North Dakota	3.5	Feb. 1983	6.8	July 2001	2.6
Ohio	9.1	Jan. 1983	13.9	Jan. 2001	3.8
Oklahoma	5.6	June 1983	9.2	Dec. 2000	2.8
Oregon	9.6	Jan. 1983	12.1	Feb. 1995	4.7
Pennsylvania	8.2	Mar. 1983	12.9	Mar. 2000	4.0
Rhode Island	10.6	Mar. 2010	11.8	July 1988	2.9
South Carolina	11.1	Dec. 2009	11.8	Mar. 1998	3.2
South Dakota	4.7	Feb. 1983	6.0	Mar. 2000	2.5
Tennessee	9.7	Jan. 1983	12.8	May 2000	3.9
Texas	8.5	Nov. 1986	9.3	Jan. 2001	4.2
Utah	7.6	Mar. 1983	10.0	Apr. 2007	2.4
Vermont	5.9	Jan. 1976	8.8	Apr. 2000	2.4
Virginia	6.3	Jan. 1983	7.8	Dec. 2000	2.2
Washington	9.3	Nov. 1982	12.2	May 2007	4.5
West Virginia	8.1	Mar. 1983	18.1	Apr. 2008	3.9
Wisconsin	7.9	Jan. 1983	11.5	Feb. 2000	3.0
Wyoming	5.8	Jan. 1987	9.1	Apr. 1979	2.3

Note: Data series begin in January 1976.

[p] = preliminary.
NOTE: Rates shown are a percentage of the labor force. Data refer to place of residence. Estimates for at least the latest five years are subject to revision early in the following calendar year. Historical highs and lows show the most recent month that a rate was recorded in the event of multiple occurrences.

Appendix B: International Unemployment Rates and Employment Indexes, Seasonally Adjusted

Summary: These are job projections mostly in Western Europe.

U.S. Department of Labor – Bureau of Labor Statistics; International Labor Organization

http://www.bls.gov/ilc/intl_unemployment_rates_monthly.htm#Rtable2

BLS: Chart 1 – Unemployment rates adjusted to U.S. concepts, 10 countries, seasonally adjusted, February 2010 – July 2011

CHART 1. Unemployment rates adjusted to U.S. concepts, 10 countries, seasonally adjusted, February 2010–July 2011

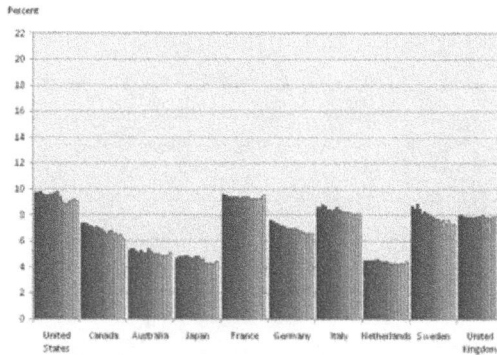

NOTE: Latest available monthly data are shown for each country. See Table 1.

BLS: Chart 2 – Unemployment rates unadjusted by BLS, 10 European Union countries or areas, seasonally adjusted, February 2010 – July 2011

CHART 2. Unemployment rates unadjusted by BLS, 10 European Union countries or areas, seasonally adjusted, February 2010–July 2011

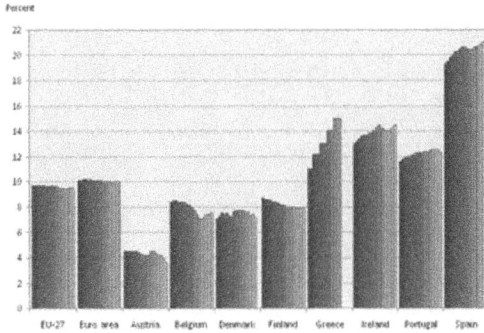

NOTE: Latest available monthly data are shown for each country except for Greece, which are for the respective quarter. See Table 2.

BLS: Table 1 – Unemployment rates adjusted to U.S. concepts, 10 countries, seasonally adjusted, February 2010 – July 2011

TABLE 1. Unemployment rates adjusted to U.S. concepts, 10 countries, seasonally adjusted (in percent)

	2007	2008	2009	2010	Q3 2010	Q4 2010	Q1 2011	Q2 2011	Jul. 2010	May 2011	Jun. 2011	Jul. 2011	Change from Jun. 2011-Jul. 2011
United States	4.6	5.8	9.3	9.6	9.6	9.6	8.9	9.1	9.5	9.1	9.2	9.1	-0.1
Australia	4.4	4.2	5.6	5.2	5.2	5.2	5.0	4.9	5.3	4.9	4.9	5.1	0.2
Canada	5.2	5.3	7.3	7.1	7.0	6.7	6.7	6.5	7.0	6.4	6.5	6.2	-0.3
France	8.1	7.5	9.2	9.4	9.4	9.4	9.3	r9.3	9.4	r9.3	r9.4	9.5	0.1
Germany (1)	8.7	7.6	7.8	7.2	7.1	7.0	6.8	6.6	7.2	6.6	6.6	6.6	0.0
Italy	6.2	6.8	7.9	8.6	8.4	8.4	8.2	8.1	8.4	8.1	8.1	8.1	0.0
Japan (2)	3.6	3.7	4.8	4.8	4.7	4.7	4.4	4.3	4.8	4.2	4.3	4.4	0.1
Netherlands	3.6	3.1	3.7	4.5	4.5	4.4	4.3	4.2	4.6	4.3	4.2	4.4	0.2
Sweden	6.1	6.0	8.2	8.3	r8.2	7.8	7.6	7.4	8.3	7.6	7.3	7.3	0.0
United Kingdom	5.4	5.7	7.7	7.9	7.8	7.9	7.8		7.8	7.9			

Footnotes:

(1) Quarterly and monthly data are calculated by applying adjustment factors to current administrative data and therefore are less precise indicators of unemployment under U.S. concepts than the annual figures.

(2) Japan data from March 2011 forward exclude approximately 5 million persons living in areas affected by the March 11 earthquake.

r = revised

NOTE: See Technical notes for information on sources and methods.

Longer time series are provided in the Excel version at www.bls.gov/ilc/intl_unemployment_rates_monthly.xls.

BLS: Table 2 – Unemployment rates unadjusted by BLS, 10 European Union countries or areas, seasonally adjusted, February 2010 – July 2011 (in percent)

TABLE 2. Unemployment rates unadjusted by BLS, 10 European Union countries or areas, seasonally adjusted
(in percent)

	2007	2008	2009	2010	Q3 2010	Q4 2010	Q1 2011	Q2 2011	Jul. 2010	May 2011	Jun. 2011	Jul. 2011	Change from Jun. 2011-Jul. 2011
EU-27 (1)	7.2	7.1	9.0	9.7	r 9.6	9.6	9.5	r 9.5	9.7	r 9.5	r 9.5	9.5	0.0
Euro area (1)	7.6	7.6	9.6	10.1	10.1	10.1	10.0	9.9	10.2	r 10.0	r 10.0	10.0	0.0
Austria	4.4	3.8	4.8	4.4	4.4	4.2	r 4.4	4.1	4.5	4.2	r 3.9	3.7	-0.2
Belgium	7.5	7.0	7.9	8.3	8.3	7.9	7.2	7.3	8.4	r 7.4	7.4	7.5	0.1
Denmark	3.8	3.3	6.0	7.4	7.4	7.7	7.6	7.3	7.3	r 7.4	7.2		
Finland	6.9	6.4	8.2	8.4	8.3	8.1	8.0	r 7.9	8.4	r 7.9	r 7.9	7.8	0.0
Greece	8.3	7.7	9.5	12.6	13.0	14.1	15.0	(2)	(2)	(2)	(2)	(2)	
Ireland	4.6	6.3	11.9	13.7	r 13.8	r 14.3	r 14.2	14.2	r 13.7	r 14.1	r 14.3	14.5	0.2
Portugal	8.9	8.5	10.6	12.0	12.2	12.3	12.4	r 12.5	12.1	r 12.6	r 12.5	12.3	-0.2
Spain	8.3	11.3	18.0	20.1	20.5	20.5	20.6	r 20.9	20.3	20.8	21.0	21.2	0.2

Footnotes:
(1) The European Union-27 (EU-27) refers to the EU member countries as of January 1, 2007. The Euro area refers to the EU member countries that adopted the euro as a common currency. See Technical notes.
(2) Data are not published on a monthly basis.

r = revised

NOTE: These data are prepared by the Statistical Office of the European Communities (EUROSTAT). See Technical notes for information on sources and methods.

Longer time series are provided in the Excel version at www.bls.gov/fls/intl_unemployment_rates_monthly.xls.

ILO: Figure 6 - Change in Labour Force Participation Rate, 2002-07 versus 2007-09, selected regions

http://www.ilo.org/wcmsp5/groups/public/@dgreports/@dcomm/@publ/documents/publication/wcms_150440.pdf

Figure 6   Change in labour force participation rate, 2002–07 versus 2007–09, selected regions

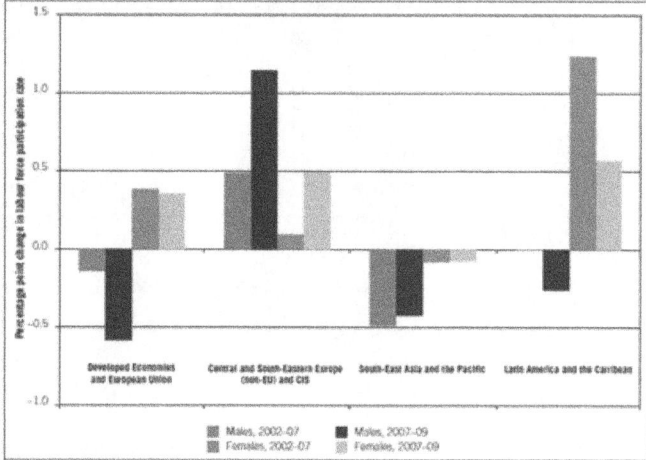

Note: 2002–07 values are average two-year trends.

Source: Calculations based on ILO, *Trends econometric models*, October 2010.

ILO: Figure 7 - Official Youth Unemployment rates and adjusted rates accounting for reduced labour force participation, 2009

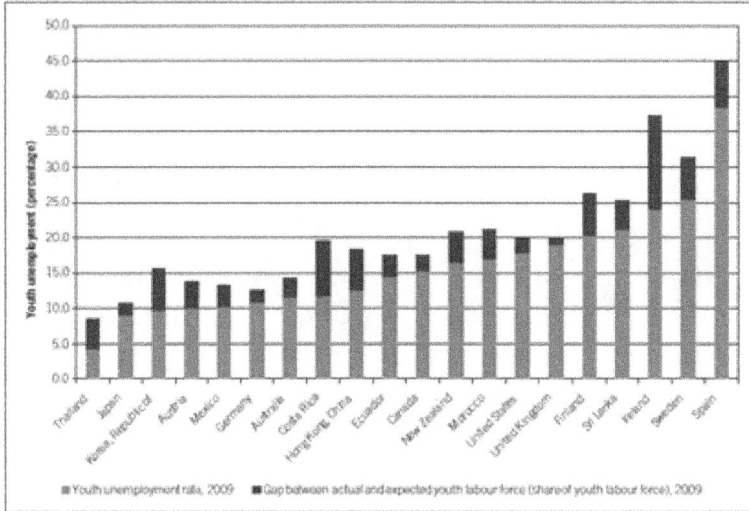

Figure 7 Official youth unemployment rates and adjusted rates accounting for reduced labour force participation, 2009

Source: Calculations based on ILO, *Trends econometric models*, October 2010.

ILO: Figure 8 - Labor productivity growth and employment growth, world and regions, 2007 and 2009

Figure 8   Labour productivity growth and employment growth, world and regions, 2007 and 2009

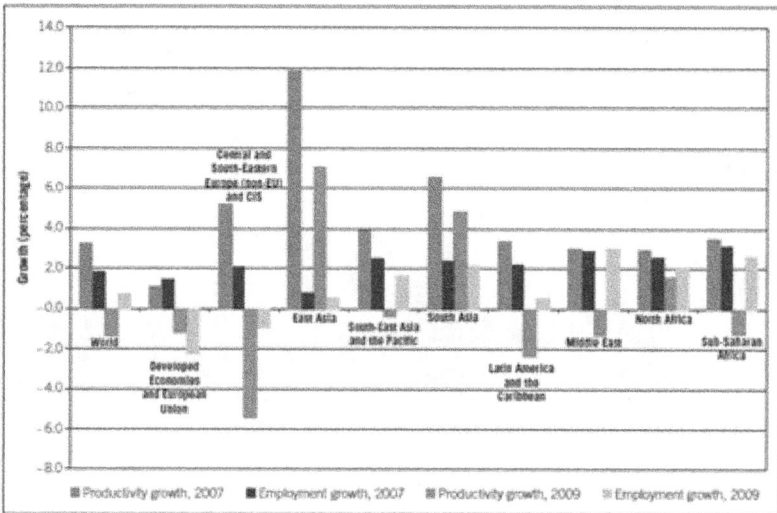

Source: ILO, *Trends econometric models*, October 2010 (see Annex 4); and World Bank, *World Development Indicators*, 2010.

ILO: Figure 9 Growth in Real GDP, employment, labour productivity and real wages, selected economies, Q1 2008-Q1 2009 and Q1 2010

Figure 9   Growth in real GDP, employment, labour productivity and real wages, selected economies, Q1 2008–Q1 2009 and Q1 2009–Q1 2010

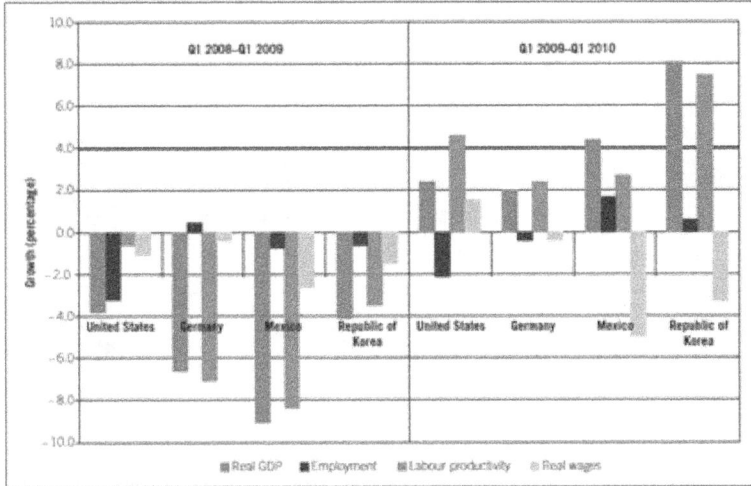

Note: Wage data correspond to annual estimates for 2008 and 2009, while other indicators correspond to annual changes from the first quarter of 2008 and 2009.

Source: Employment, GDP and productivity: calculations based on national data; real wages: ILO, *Global Wage Report 2010/11*.

ILO: Figure 11 - Employment by sector, world and labor selected regions, average annual percentage change 2002-07 and 2008-09

Figure 11 Employment by sector, world and selected regions, average annual percentage change 2002–07 and 2008–09

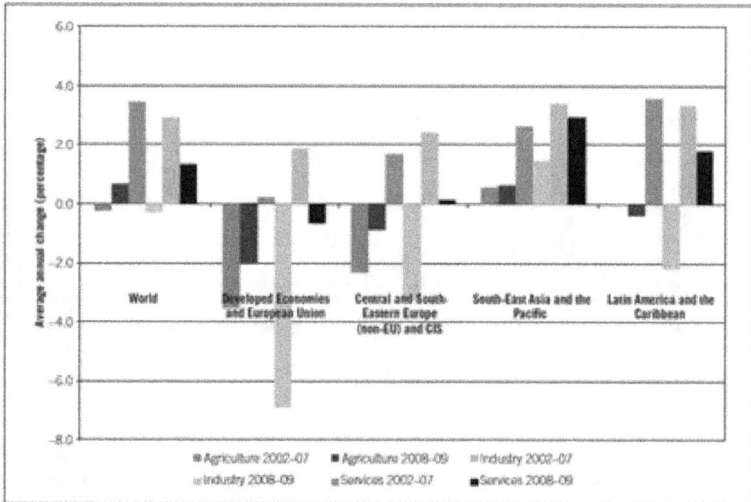

Source: ILO, *Trends econometric models*, October 2010 (see Annex 4).

ILO: Figure 15 - Annual change in employment, selected economies, 2007-09 (annual average) and 2009-10

TABLE 3. Employment indexes adjusted to U.S. concepts, 10 countries, seasonally adjusted

	Q3 2010	Q4 2010	Q1 2011	Q2 2011	Jul. 2010	May 2011	Jun. 2011	Jul. 2011	Change from Jun. 2011-Jul. 2011
	Q3 2010 = 100				Jul. 2010 = 100				
United States	100.0	99.9	100.3	100.3	100.0	100.6	100.2	100.2	0.0
Australia	100.0	100.9	101.2	101.3	100.0	101.5	101.7	101.7	0.0
Canada	100.0	100.1	100.8	101.2	100.0	101.2	101.4	101.5	0.1
France	100.0	99.1	100.1	99.6	(1)	(1)	(1)	(1)	
Germany	100.0	100.3	100.7	101.0	100.0	101.1	101.3	101.3	0.0
Italy	100.0	100.2	100.2	100.3	100.0	100.3	100.2	100.4	0.2
Japan	100.0	100.0	(2)	(2)	100.0	(2)	(2)	(2)	
Netherlands	100.0	100.2	99.9	99.7	100.0	99.5	99.9	99.7	-0.2
Sweden	100.0	100.8	101.5	101.8	100.0	101.6	101.9	101.6	-0.3
United Kingdom	100.0	99.9	100.3		100.0	100.4			

Footnotes:

(1) Data are not published on a monthly basis.

(2) Data for Japan are not available as of March 2011, as monthly figures published by the Japan Statistics Bureau now exclude approximately 5 million persons living in areas affected by the March 11 earthquake.

NOTE: See Technical notes for information on sources and methods.

Longer time series are provided in the Excel version at www.bls.gov/ilc/intl_unemployment_rates_monthly.xls.

Figure 15   Annual change in employment, selected economies, 2007–09 (annual average) and 2009–10

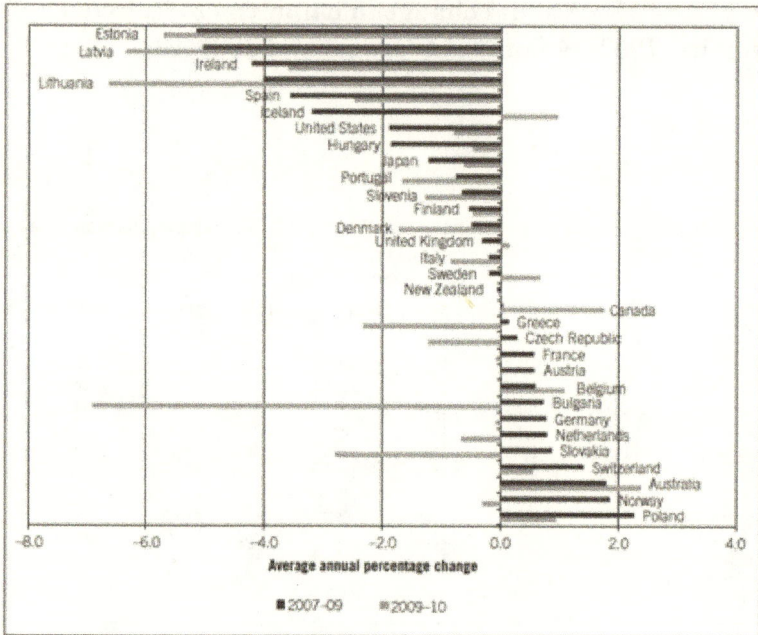

Average annual percentage change

■ 2007–09   ▥ 2009–10

Note: Based on data from second quarter in each year.

Source: National statistical offices.

Appendix C: Verses to Cheer You Up

Summary: These are motivational verses and quotes.

I acknowledge the wisdom articulated by known and unknown authors in the following verses. Note: for verses with unknown sources, reasonable effort and time were spent to trace the authors.

Verses: Steve Jobs' 2005 Stanford University Commencement Address

http://www.youtube.com/watch?v=UF8uR6Z6KLc

http://news.stanford.edu/news/2005/june15/jobs-061505.html

Verses: The Psalms 23

The LORD is my shepherd; I shall not want.

He maketh me to lie down in green pastures:
    he leadeth me beside the still waters.

He restoreth my soul:
    he leadeth me in the paths of righteousness for his name's sake.

Yea, though I walk through the valley of the shadow of death,
    I will fear no evil: for thou art with me;
thy rod and thy staff they comfort me.

Thou preparest a table before me in the presence of mine enemies:
    thou anointest my head with oil;
my cup runneth over.

Surely goodness and mercy shall follow me all the days of my life:
    and I will dwell in the house of the LORD for ever.

- Author: The Bible

Verses: Ecclesiastes 3

To every thing there is a season, and a time to every purpose
under the heaven:
A time to be born, and a time to die; time to plant, and a time
to pluck up that which is planted;

A time to kill, and a time to heal; a time to break down, and a
time to build up;

A time to weep, and a time to laugh; a time to mourn, and a time
to dance;

A time to cast away stones, and a time to gather stones together;
a time to embrace, and a time to refrain from embracing;

A time to get, and a time to lose; a time to keep, and a time to
cast away;

A time to rend, and a time to sew; a time to keep silence, and a
time to speak;

A time to love, and a time to hate; a time of war, and a time of
peace.

- Author: The Bible

Verses: You'll Never Walk Alone

http://www.risa.co.uk/sla/song.php?songid=16078

When you walk through a storm
Hold your head up high
And don't be afraid of the dark

At the end of the storm
Is a golden sky
And the sweet silver song of the lark

Walk on through the wind
Walk on through the rain
Though your dreams be tossed and blown

Walk on walk on with hope in your heart
And you'll never walk alone
You'll never walk alone

When you walk through a storm
Hold your head up high
And don't be afraid of the dark

At the end of the storm
Is a golden sky
And the sweet silver song of the lark

Walk on through the wind
Walk on through the rain
Though your dreams be tossed and blown

Walk on walk on with hope in your heart
And you'll never walk alone
You'll never walk

You'll never walk
You'll never walk alone.

- Author: Rodgers and Hammerstein

Verses: A Dinner of Thanksgiving

She was just a bent old lady
Her hair was full of gray
I was just a child of seven
Who had stepped outside to play.

Her dress was worn and tattered
She looked so frail and thin
But her eyes were warm and caring
And she kindly asked me in.

As the morning hours were fading
I recall her gentle plea
"Please stay a little longer
And enjoy a meal with me."

I had no way of knowing
That her shelves were nearly bare
But it didn't really matter
She was glad to have me there.

The meal was small and meager
But I felt like I'd been blessed
When I sat there at the table
And she served to me her best.

In honor of her memory
This moment I will seize
To be thankful for the bounty
When we shared a bowl of peas.

I am humbled by her spirit
Unblemished through the years
She's smiling down from heaven
As I wipe away these tears.

For she, too, still remembers
That warm delightful day
When a little girl of seven
Had stepped outside to play.

Have a blessed Thanksgiving!!!

- Author: Unknown

Verses: If The Earth was a Village

If we could shrink the earth's population to village of precisely 100 people, with all the existing human ratio remaining the same, it would look something like the following:

There would be:

- 57 Asians
- 21 Europeans
- 14 from the Western Hemisphere, both north and south
- 8 Africans

- 52 would be female
- 48 would be male
- 70 would be non-white
- 30 would be white
- 70 would be non-Christian
- 30 would be Christian
- 89 would be heterosexual
- 11 would be homosexual
- 6 people would possess 59% of the entire world's wealth and all 6 would be from the United States.
- 80 would live in substandard housing
- 70 would be unable to read
- 50 would suffer from malnutrition
- 1 would be near death
- 1 would be near birth
- 1 (yes, only 1) would have a college education
- 1 would own a computer

When one considers our world from such a compressed perspective, the need for acceptance, understanding and education becomes glaringly apparent.

The following is also something to ponder...

If you woke up this morning with more health than illness...you are more blessed than many others. If you have never experienced the danger of battle, the loneliness of imprisonment, the agony of torture, or the pangs of starvation...you are ahead of 500 million people in the world.

If you can attend a church meeting without fear of harassment, arrest, torture, or death...you are more blessed than three billion people in the world.

If you have food in the refrigerator, clothes on your back, a roof overhead and a place to sleep...you are richer than 75% of this world.

If you have money in the bank, in your wallet, and spare change in a dish someplace ... you are among the top 8% of the world's wealthy.

If your parents are still alive and still married ... you are very rare, even in the United States and Canada.

If you can read this message, you are more blessed than over two billion people in the world that cannot read at all.

Someone once said: What goes around comes around.

Work like you don't need the money.
Love like you've never been hurt.
Dance like nobody's watching.
Sing like nobody's listening.
Live like it's Heaven on Earth.

- Author: Unknown

Verses: 1000 Marbles

http://www.naute.com/stories/marbles.phtml

The older I get, the more I enjoy Saturday mornings. Perhaps it's the quiet solitude that comes with being the first to rise, or maybe it's the unbounded joy of not having to be at work. Either way, the first few hours of a Saturday morning are most enjoyable. A few weeks ago, I was shuffling toward the basement shack with a steaming cup of coffee in one hand and the morning paper in the other. What began as a typical Saturday morning, turned into one of those lessons that life seems to hand you from time to time.

Let me tell you about it.

I turned the dial up into the phone portion of the band on my ham radio in order to listen to a Saturday morning swap net. Along the way, I came across an older sounding chap, with a tremendous signal and a golden voice. You know the kind, he sounded like he should be in the broadcasting business. He was telling whoever he was talking with something about "a thousand marbles".

I was intrigued and stopped to listen to what he had to say. "Well, Tom, it sure sounds like you're busy with your job. I'm sure they pay you well but it's a shame you have to be away from home and your family so much. Hard to believe a young fellow should have to work sixty or seventy hours a week to make ends meet. Too bad you missed your daughter's dance recital."

He continued, "let me tell you something Tom, something that has helped me keep a good perspective on my own priorities."

And that's when he began to explain his theory of a "thousand marbles."

"You see, I sat down one day and did a little arithmetic. The average person lives about seventy-five years. I know, some live more and some live less, but on average, folks live about seventy-five years."

"Now then, I multiplied 75 times 52 and I came up with 3900 which is the number of Saturdays that the average person has in their entire lifetime. Now stick with me Tom, I'm getting to the important part."

"It took me until I was fifty-five years old to think about all this in any detail", he went on, "and by that time I had lived through over twenty-eight hundred Saturdays. I got to thinking that if I lived to be seventy-five, I only had about a thousand of them left to enjoy."

"So I went to a toy store and bought every single marble they had. I ended up having to visit three toy stores to round-up 1000 marbles. I took them home and put them inside of a large, clear plastic container right here in the shack next to my gear."

"Every Saturday since then, I have taken one marble out and thrown it away."

"I found that by watching the marbles diminish, I focused more on the really important things in life. There is nothing like watching your time here on this earth run out to help get your priorities straight."

"Now let me tell you one last thing before I sign-off with you and take my lovely wife out for breakfast. This morning, I took the very last marble out of the container. I figure if I make it until next Saturday then I have been given a little extra time. And the one thing we can all use is a little more time."

"It was nice to meet you Tom, I hope you spend more time with your family, and I hope to meet you again here on the band. 73 Old Man, this is K9NZQ, clear and going QRT, good morning!"

You could have heard a pin drop on the band when this fellow signed off. I guess he gave us all a lot to think about.

I had planned to work on the antenna that morning, and then I was going to meet up with a few hams to work on the next club newsletter.

Instead, I went upstairs and woke my wife up with a kiss. "C'mon honey, I'm taking you and the kids to breakfast."

"What brought this on?" she asked with a smile.

"Oh, nothing special, it's just been a long time since we spent a Saturday together with the kids. Hey, can we stop at a toy store while we're out? I need to buy some marbles."

- Author: Jeffrey Davis

Verses: Trust

TRUST...
"It takes years to build trust and a few seconds to destroy it"

VALUE...
"What is most valuable is not what you have in your life but who you have in
your life".

MONEY...
"Money can buy everything but happiness".

DON'T HURT ANYBODY...

"It only takes a few seconds to hurt people you love, and it can take years to
heal".

LIVE TODAY...
There are two eternities that can break you down. Yesterday and Tomorrow. One is gone and the other doesn't exist... So live today".

MARRIAGE...
Do not marry a person that you know that you can live with; only marry someone
that you cannot live without".

SHARERS...
"A successful relationship is not built on givers and takers only, but on people
who also become sharers".

- Author: Unknown

Verses: Peace Be Dine

God looked around his Garden and found an empty place.
He then looked down upon his earth and saw your loving face.

He put his arms around you and lifted you to rest.
His Garden must be beautiful, he always takes the best.
He knew that you were suffering, he knew you were in pain.
And knew that you would never get well on earth again.
He saw your path was difficult, he closed you tired eyes,
He whispered to you "Peace be Thine" and gave you wings to fly.
When we saw you sleeping so calm and free of pain,
We would not wish you back to earth to suffer once again.
You've left us precious memories, your love will be our guide,
You live on through your children, you're always by our side.
It broke our hearts to lose you, but you did not go alone.
For part of us went with you on the day God called you home

- Author: Unknown

Verses: Do Not Stand and Weep

Do not stand at my grave and weep.
I am not there.
I do not sleep

I am a thousand winds that swiftly blow.
I am the diamond glint
on newly fallen snow.
I am the sunlight
on ripened grain.
I am the soft and gentle autumn rain

When you wake from sleep in the early morning hush,
I am the swift, uplifting rush
of quiet birds in circling flight.
I am the soft, starlight at night.

Do not stand at my grave and weep.
I am not there.
I do not sleep.

- Author: Unknown

Verses: Other Motivational Verses

http://www.inspirational-quotes.info/

http://heartsandminds.org/quotes/quotes.htm

Appendix D: Movies to Cheer You Up

Summary: These are motivational movies.

Movie: Sound of Music starring Julie Andrews and Christopher Plummer

http://www.the-sound-of-music-guide.com/sound-of-music-cast.html

Movie: Don Juan de Marco starring Johnny Depp

http://en.wikipedia.org/wiki/Don_Juan_DeMarco

Movie: A Walk in the Clouds starring Keanu Reeves

http://en.wikipedia.org/wiki/A_Walk_in_the_Clouds

Movie: Thomas Kinkade's "Christmas Cottage (Home for Christmas) starring Peter O'Toole

http://www.thomaskinkade.com/magi/servlet/com.asucon.ebiz. promo.web.tk.PromoServlet?promoAction=chrcot

Movie: About Schmidt starring Jack Nicholson

http://en.wikipedia.org/wiki/About_Schmidt

http://en.wikipedia.org/wiki/Foster_care

http://en.wikipedia.org/wiki/Orphanage

http://volunteerguide.org/volunteer/vacation/orphanages.htm?g clid=CIyPguun3KsCFSOAgwodLntmPQ

http://www.orphanage.org/

http://www.missionfinder.org/orphanages.htm

Movie: Johnny Carson's The Tonight Show Reruns

http://www.imdb.com/name/nm0001992/

Movie: Seven Samurais - Akira Kurozawa & Toshiro Mifune

http://en.wikipedia.org/wiki/Seven_Samurai

http://www.albany.edu/writers-inst/webpages4/filmnotes/fns04n4.html

Movie: Hereafter with Matt Damon and Cécile de France

http://en.wikipedia.org/wiki/Hereafter_(film)

Movie: Pay It Forward with Helen Hunt and Kevin Spacey

http://en.wikipedia.org/wiki/Pay_It_Forward

Movie: Book of Eli with Denzel Washington

http://en.wikipedia.org/wiki/The_Book_of_Eli

Appendix E: Music to Cheer You Up

Summary: These are motivational musical pieces.

Music: What a Wonderful World – Louis Armstrong

> http://www.youtube.com/watch?v=SzJY96m3lkg

Music: Sound of Music starring Julie Andrews and Christopher Plummer

> http://www.youtube.com/watch?v=KuWsQSntFf0

Music: You'll Never Walk Alone – The Mormon Tabernacle Choir

> http://www.youtube.com/watch?v=YMy_oSeK5JE

Music: The Impossible Dream – Luther Vandross

> http://www.youtube.com/watch?v=cGsYrpejAYw

Music: Somewhere in the Rainbow – Israel Kamakawiwo'ole

> http://www.youtube.com/watch?v=V1bFr2SWP1I

Music: First of May – Sarah Brightman

> http://www.youtube.com/watch?v=kjEwqpyzU1k

Music: Greenfields - Brothers Four

> http://www.youtube.com/watch?v=cYD3pkbgnKA

Music: A House is Not a Home - Luther Vandross

> http://www.youtube.com/watch?v=Gu2JBMNBbKo

Music: Meditation - Massenet (Meditation from Thais)

http://www.youtube.com/watch?v=PGd4Rs-O3ws&feature=related

http://www.youtube.com/watch?v=Ss1URTJYlfQ&feature=related

http://www.youtube.com/watch?v=_ajCJFgbsFs&feature=related

Music: Other Motivational Music

http://celestinechua.com/blog/inspirational-songs/

http://www.goal-setting-college.com/motivation/inspirational-motivational-songs/

Appendix F: Job Search Resources

Summary: These are job search tools.

Job Search Engines

2011 guide to the top 100 US job search categories. For each top employment category it lists the top 3 or 4 niche job search websites

http://www.internetinc.com/job-search-websites/

Monster is one of the largest job search engine in the world, with over a million job postings at any time and over 150 million resumes, in the database and over 63 million job seekers per month. The company employs approximately 5,000 employees in 36 countries.

http://www.monster.com/

Job markets across the world

http://www.job.com/

Job markets across the world

http://www.alljobsearch.com/

Indeed.com is a metasearch engine for job listings launched in November 2004. As a single-topic search engine, it is also an example of vertical search. The site aggregates job listings from thousands of websites, including job boards, newspapers, associations, and company career pages. Job seekers do not apply for jobs through Indeed; they simply see job postings. Applicants can then decide which jobs are of interest and then go to the corresponding sites to apply. Indeed is currently available in 53 countries.

http://www.indeed.com/

Website for temporary workers

http://www.net-temps.com/

CareerBuilder.com is the largest online employment website in the United States, with more than 23 million unique visitors each month and a 34% market share of help-wanted web sites in the United States.[2] CareerBuilder.com provides online career search services for more than 1,900 partners as of March 2008, including 140 newspapers and portals such as AOL and MSN.

http://www.careerbuilder.com/

Simply Hired is a metasearch engine for job listings (thus also an example of vertical search) and online recruitment advertising network. The company aggregates job listings from thousands of sites across the Web including job boards, newspaper and classified listings, associations, social networks, content sites and company career sites. It then distributes those jobs on SimplyHired.com, and its 5,000 social network, media content, blog, and niche website partners.

http://www.simplyhired.com/

U.S. Federal government online job database

http://www.usajobs.gov/

Search engine for 11,000 career sites around the country including college, university and military offices.

http://www.collegerecruiter.com/

California Job Search website

http://www.jobbankusa.com/jobs/california_ca/job_e
mployment_search.html

U.S. Department of Labor

http://www.dol.gov/ebsa/cobra.html

California Employment Development

http://www.caljobs.ca.gov/

California Job Openings

http://www.california.jobopenings.net/

http://www.careerprofiles.info/california-job-sites.html

http://www.realcaliforniajobs.com/

Jobs in 50 states

http://50statejobs.com/

http://govcareers.about.com/od/JobSearch/tp/Job-Boards-For-All-50-States.htm

State Employment Sites for 50 states

http://www.statelocalgov.net/50states-jobs.cfm

Jobs for Seniors

http://www.workforce50.com/

http://seniorjobs.org/

California Unemployment Insurance

http://www.edd.ca.gov/unemployment/

Unemployment Insurance in 50 states

http://www.layoffsurvivalplan.com/resources/unemployment-benefits-websites.html

Employment Resources for Non-Profits

http://www.employmentresourcesinc.org/

Employment Resources for Ex-Offenders

http://www.iseek.org/guide/exoffenders/index.html

Resources for Self-Employed

http://www.usa.gov/Business/Self_Employed.shtml

Employment Resources For the Disabled and Those with Special Needs

http://www.dol.gov/odep/

https://www.disability.gov/employment

http://www.protectyourincome.com/education-center/disability-insurance-tip-center/employment-resources-for-the-disabled

http://www.disabledonline.com/link-directory/employment/

COBRA program

http://www.dol.gov/ebsa/cobra.html

Renegotiate Healthcare bills

http://www. healthcarebluebook.com

http://www.nytimes.com/2009/03/14/health/14patient.html

http://magazine.angieslist.com/doctors/articles/negotiating-health-care-bills-a-growing-trend.aspx

http://frugalliving.about.com/od/beautyhealthcare/a/How-To-Negotiate-Your-Medical-Bills.htm

Resume Writing Skills

http://owl.english.purdue.edu/owl/resource/626/01/

http://jobsearch.about.com/b/2011/08/26/resume-skills.htm

Interview Skills

http://www.career.vt.edu/interviewing/Index.html

http://en.wikipedia.org/wiki/Job_interview

http://jobsearch.about.com/od/interviewsnetworking/a/wininterview.htm

Appendix G: Une journée dans la vie d'un imbécile: 8/26/2011

Summary: This is an example of reaching out to learn another culture and perspective.

From: David Paraiso
Date: 2011/8/26
Subject: Une Journée dans la vie d'un Imbécile: 8/26/2011
To: File

I took my lunch at the Himalaya Café (http://www.himalayancafela.com/) – they specialize on Nepalese Indian and Tibetan cuisines. This is across All-India Café and Culture 21 along Fair Oaks. It is scorching hot today, like being inside an oven.

My colleague and friend Shu Zhang from China was the one who introduced me to this restaurant the other Friday - as part of our once a week program of learning and immersing ourselves in other cultures.

I like the food – Naan (leaven tandoor baked bread; refer to http://en.wikipedia.org/wiki/Naan); mild curry on chicken; fried chicken; vegetable; dessert; and, tea with cinnamon. I will come here again…

There are pictures of:

- Kathmandu

  http://en.wikipedia.org/wiki/Kathmandu

- Bouddhanatah

  http://en.wikipedia.org/wiki/Boudhanath

  http://wikitravel.org/en/Boudhanath

  http://www.keithdowman.net/books/bgs.htm

- Nepal

  http://en.wikipedia.org/wiki/Nepal

Someday, I would like to travel sections of the Silk Road (http://en.wikipedia.org/wiki/Silk_Road) – between the steps of Mongolia all the way to India and Europe.

This is part of my personal journey in finding out more and understanding various religions, cultures and the world.

Appendix H: Expand Your Horizon

Summary: these are materials providing perspectives from various sources.

Horizon: Great Courses

http://www.thegreatcourses.com/

Horizon: Tipping Point

http://www.wikisummaries.org/The_Tipping_Point

Horizon: Best Sellers - All Time

http://www.wikisummaries.org/Category:Bestsellers

Horizon: Book Summaries

http://www.wikisummaries.org/Category:Summaries

Horizon: Best Sellers - Barnes and Noble

http://www.barnesandnoble.com/u/Bestseller-Books/379001057/

Horizon: Best Sellers - Amazon

http://www.amazon.com/best-sellers-books-Amazon/zgbs/books

Horizon: Best Sellers - New York Times

http://www.nytimes.com/best-sellers-books/overview.html

Horizon: Best Sellers - USA Today

http://books.usatoday.com/list/index

Horizon: National Public Radio

> http://www.npr.org/

Horizon: C-Span

> http://www.c-span.org/

Horizon: Greed

> http://www.cnbc.com/id/32210731/

> http://www.cnbc.com/id/29894073/

> http://tv.msn.com/tv/series-episodes/american-greed/

> http://articles.moneycentral.msn.com/News/CorporateGreed.as
> px

Horizon: Fraud

> http://www.consumerfraudreporting.org/

> http://www.fraud.org/

> http://www.fraudguides.com/consumer_fraud_main.asp

> https://www.ftccomplaintassistant.gov/

> http://www.consumerfraudreporting.org/stateattorneygenerallist
> .php

Horizon: Investigative Reporting

> http://www.pbs.org/wnet/expose/

> http://www.pbs.org/mediashift/2008/04/examples-of-online-
> investigative-journalism116.html

> http://centerforinvestigativereporting.org/

http://www.pbs.org/wgbh/pages/frontline/view/

http://www.ire.org/

http://www.pulitzer.org/citation/2011-Investigative-Reporting

http://www.muckraker.org/

http://www.gao.gov/